AMERICA THE MIDDLEBROW

AMERICA *the* MIDDLEBROW

Women's Novels, Progressivism, and Middlebrow Authorship between the Wars

Jaime Harker

University of Massachusetts Press
Amherst and Boston

Printed in the United States of America

LC 2007004497
ISBN 978-1-55849-597-5 (paper); 596-8 (library cloth)

Designed by Kristina Kachele Design Ltd.
Set in Cycles Eleven and Nine, Franklin Gothic Book, by dix! Digital Prepress
Printed and bound by The Maple-Vail Book Manufacturing Group

Library of Congress Cataloging-in-Publication Data
Harker, Jaime.
America the middlebrow : women's novels, progressivism,
and middlebrow authorship between the wars / Jaime Harker.
p. cm.—(Studies in print culture and the history of the book)
Includes bibliographical references (p.) and index.
ISBN 978-1-55849-596-8 (lib. bdg. : alk. paper)—ISBN 978-1-55849-597-5 (pbk. : alk. paper)
1. American fiction—Women authors—History and criticism.
2. American fiction—20th century—History and criticism.
3. Progressivism in literature. 4. Sentimentalism in literature.
5. Fisher, Dorothy Canfield, 1879–1958—Criticism and interpretation.
6. Fauset, Jessie Redmon—Criticism and interpretation.
7. Buck, Pearl S. (Pearl Sydenstricker), 1892–1973—Criticism and interpretation.
8. Herbst, Josephine, 1892–1969—Criticism and interpretation.
9. Popular literature—United States—History and criticism.
10. Women and literature—United States—History—20th century.
I. Title.
PS374.W6H37 2007
813'.52099287—dc22 2007004497

British Library Cataloguing in Publication data are available.

Contents

Acknowledgments

For nuturing this project in its early stages, I am grateful to Miles Orvell, Rachel Blau DuPlessis, Carolyn Karcher, Robert Caserio, and Laura Levitt. Miles Orvell has been an ideal mentor, giving me a model of scholarship that continues to guide me.

Many institutions have helped support the development of this manuscript. A 1997 seminar on the history of the book at the American Antiquarian Society, facilitated by Joan Shelley Rubin and Meredith McGill, influenced my work in its inception, and provided me with a community of scholars on which I continue to depend, including Erin Smith, Ellen Gruber Garvey, Catherine Turner, and Melissa Homestead, and through them, Jennifer Parchesky and Julia Ehrhardt. With the aid of a year-long American dissertation fellowship from the American Association of University Women I was able to work on the project full time, and I was able to complete it with help of a fellowship from Temple University. At the University of Mississippi I have found a supportive and colleagial community, and I thank the College of Liberal Arts for awarding me a Faculty Summer Research Grant to make final revisions on the manuscript.

Many friends have read part or all of this manuscript at some stage and shared their criticisms with me. Thanks to Erin Smith, Melissa Bradshaw,

Alida Moore, Annette Trefzer, Kathryn McKee, Karen Raber, Edward Gutting, Angela Hornsby, Mark Dolan, and especially Juli Parrish.

I would like to offer my thanks to Paul Wright, senior editor, Bruce Wilcox, director, and Carol Betsch, managing editor, at the University of Massachusetts Press, and to the outside reviewers for their helpful comments. One reviewer's insight about Harriet Beecher Stowe's charge to the reader to "feel right" helped me frame the introduction.

I am grateful to the following institutions for allowing me access to their special collections: Yale University, Columbia University, the University of Vermont, the University of Pennsylvania, Princeton University, the University of Massachusetts, Howard University, Brandt and Hochman Literary Agency, and the Library of Congress.

My parents and siblings have sustained me emotionally, and, at times, financially, over the years I have been at work on this book. Finally, I want to express my love and gratitude to my family: Alida, Grace, William, and Jack.

AMERICA THE MIDDLEBROW

Introduction

A Genealogy of Political Domestic Fiction

In 1942, Sinclair Lewis wrote approving prefatory remarks to Paxton Hibben's debunking biography of Henry Ward Beecher, the antebellum abolitionist preacher who, Lewis believed, bore a striking resemblance to his own Elmer Gantry. In an aside, Lewis sums up Beecher's more famous sister, Harriet Beecher Stowe, pithily: "*Uncle Tom's Cabin* was the first evidence to America that no hurricane can be so disastrous to a country as a ruthlessly humanitarian woman" (Lewis, Foreword x).

"Ruthlessly humanitarian." The phrase humorously juxtaposes callousness and benevolence, equating firm conviction and literary activism with a natural disaster. It is a blithe dismissal of a figure whom contemporary feminist scholars have shown to be complex, sophisticated, and innovative (Tompkins 125, Hedrick viii). For Lewis, Stowe's legacy was defined solely by her frank social advocacy in fictional form.

Uncle Tom's Cabin personalizes a complex political and social issue through vivid characterization. Stowe ends her novel with a direct appeal to readers to act upon the emotions her novel inspires: "But, what can any individual do? Of that, every individual can judge. There is one thing that every individual can do,—they can see to it that *they feel right*. An atmosphere of sympathetic influence encircles every human being; and the man or woman who *feels* strongly, healthily and justly, on the great interests of humanity, is a constant benefactor to the human race. See, then, to your sympathies in this matter!" (512). Stowe's faith in emotion and in the power of the individual to challenge injustice marks many sentimental women writers of the 1850s. *Uncle Tom's Cabin* was credited with inflaming Northern public sentiment against slavery and causing civil war. It is seen, in other words, as one of the most successful political novels ever written. Dig deeper, and Lewis's breezy dismissal of Harriet Beecher Stowe extends to political activism, socially committed novels, and women. Stowe is both symptom and symbol; women *like her,* Lewis suggests, have ruined American culture.

Debates about the past, of course, are very much about the present. Lewis's warning about the dangers of women reflects a larger cultural anxiety between the the two World Wars. Numerous feminist critics, from Bonnie Kime Scott and Rachel Blau DuPlessis to Sandra Gilbert and Susan Gubar, have critiqued the pervasive gender anxieties of the modern era, anxieties that made "effeminate" so pervasive an insult that women writers used it against other writers, both male and female. American modernist writers blamed women for American standardization, religious intolerance, racism, poor taste, and ineffectual liberal reform (Douglas 6–7).

All women writers in the twenties and thirties had to confront this new cultural scapegoating. Some, like Dorothy Parker, proved that they were as unsentimental and ruthless as the men. Those who succeeded within the emerging modernist aesthetic, like Willa Cather, obscured their connections with identifiable networks of women writers (Williams 89). The "ruthlessly humanitarian" were laughed at, vilified, blamed, dismissed. Modern American literary critics have, by and large, maintained these oppositions, elevating the writers they favor from middle-class mediocrity to modern rebellion.

Despite her clear sympathy for the modernist enterprise in her germinal book *Terrible Honesty: Mongrel Manhattan in the Twenties,* Ann Douglas concedes that "the matrophobia of the moderns was not only unfair to the Victorian women it criticized but ambivalent and unresolved, complicated by issues of gender and race difference, and blind to the psychological consequences such resistance entails" (8). Luckily, however, "Victorian matriarchs" spoke for themselves in the twenties and thirties, embracing emotion and activism through the literary marketplace.

This book investigates women writers of the interwar period who challenged their own generation of Americans to "feel right," and argues that they represent a heretofore invisible category of American authorship. The 1850s and the 1970s have both been studied extensively as moments when women writers merged activism and literature. First and second wave feminism have been separated, in the critical imagination, by a fallow period in women's activist writing. *America the Middlebrow* proposes a link, positing a school of activist fiction embracing four writers who have been considered, when considered at all, as anomalies or flukes.

The connections among these four writers—Dorothy Canfield, Jessie Fauset, Pearl Buck, and Josephine Herbst—are not obvious. They would not have imagined themselves as part of a unified group; though Canfield and Buck were friends, Fauset and Herbst would not have recognized a common bond. Canfield and Buck were magazine and Book-of-the-Month-Club writers, and participants in individual political causes; Fauset was active with the National Association for the Advancement of Colored People and in the "New Negro" literary movement; Herbst, a modern rebel employed by H. L. Mencken in the twenties, became a proletarian writer in the thirties.

And yet, when one considers these authors together, one discovers interlocking concerns and shared interests. All worked from older models of authorship and eschewed dramatic formal experimentation; all were interested in using their fiction to persuade their audience of left-leaning political positions; all wanted to find a wide readership in the burgeoning literary marketplace; and all were at various times denigrated by male critics as middle-class, "feminine," and sentimental.

All four shaped their writing and its content to their understanding of a women's readership. All four concealed information about their own lives in order to reach what they considered a "mainstream" audience; the key issue was sex. Fauset's affair with the married W. E. B. Du Bois, Buck's interracial affair with the Chinese poet Xu Zhimo, and Herbst's affair with the painter Marion Greenwood—none of these illicit alliances appeared in their fiction. Canfield, Fauset, Buck, and Herbst placated certain assumptions in their readers in order to challenge others. Dorothy Canfield explored a woman's adulterous feelings and denounced racism as un-American in a novel about romantic love triangles. Jessie Fauset countered the sexual stereotyping of African Americans with her images of a thoroughly conventional black middle class. Pearl Buck presented unconventional sexual and religious mores *and* challenged American stereotypes about the "Orient." Josephine Herbst rewrote radicalism as profoundly American in relating the decline of a white, middle-class Midwestern family. All four of these writers demonstrate both a faith in common readers and a desire to educate and improve them; Canfield and Buck emphasized the former, Fauset and Herbst the latter.

Canfield and Buck were widely read. Herbst and Fauset had more modest sales, but each is representative of interwar literary culture; if they didn't personally gain large readerships, as Canfield and Buck did, their writing was part of an influential trend during the interwar period. In the following chapters I trace the evolution of this mode of authorship, focusing on key points throughout the twenties and thirties. Canfield's *Brimming Cup* provided a middlebrow counterpoint to post–World War I modernist rebellion, especially that of Sinclair Lewis in 1921. Jessie Fauset's *There Is Confusion* introduced the Harlem Renaissance in 1924. Pearl Buck tapped into contemporary interest in novels of the soil and in international politics with *The Good Earth* in 1931; and Josephine Herbst exemplified the publishing trend of the proletarian novel with *The Executioner Waits* in 1934. My account of these four writers takes us through the twenties and thirties up to the height of the Popular Front.

Only when one reads these four authors together do their convergences become clear. Collectively, they define a distinct category of authorship; individually, each extends the boundaries of that category. But though they differed in strategy and emphasis, each insisted on the importance of activism and progressive commitment in their fiction.

Before turning to more detailed analysis, I want to outline the larger tradition of political domestic fiction, one that begins with "sentimental power" in the 1850s, continues through the Progressive era, notably in "pragmatist aesthetics," and is seen in the interwar period under the rubric "middlebrow." Each generation of writers modifies it, but an identifiable tradition of women's activist writing continues from the 1850s to the interwar period—and beyond. Canfield, Fauset, Buck, and Herbst embody the intersection of women's novels, progressivism, and middlebrow authorship in the interwar period.

Sentimental Power: Women Activist Writers of the 1850s

Until the 1970s, women novelists of the 1850s had been dismissed as "sentimental" writers unworthy of serious critical attention. Second wave feminist scholarship radically reformulated assumptions about the nineteenth century, about women, and about the appropriate means to political power. Feminist critics have reclaimed sentimental, reform-minded nineteenth-century fiction as complex literary productions worthy of serious attention.[1] In turn, twentieth-century interwar activist writers have become visible as part of an ongoing tradition. Nina Baym's *Woman's Fiction* defines some key terms and identifies characteristics that are particularly relevant to my study.

Baym explains that writers of "woman's fiction" considered themselves "professional writers with work to do and a living to be made from satisfactory fulfillment of an obligation to their audience" (16). Fulfilling that obligation, in fact, seemed to be their primary goal; all other considerations, including plots and stylistic choices, were secondary. Their readership, primarily middle-class white women, wanted to be entertained as well as "to take away something from their reading that would help them in their lives" (16–17). Sentimental women writers therefore constructed recognizable plots that, despite dramatic turns, always ended with the triumph of the heroine. The exemplary heroine was the key to readers' pleasure, their emotional experience, and their education; sentimental writers succeeded "by engaging and channeling the emotions of readers through identification with the heroine" (17). The formal and thematic choices that made this identification easy also made women's fiction a financial and cultural success.

Baym suggests that women's fiction did do significant political and cultural work: it provided images of female autonomy. It was, however, an "unspectacular" feminism, neither systematic nor radical. Its writers "interpreted experience within models of personal relations, rather than classes, castes, or other institutional structures" (18). In the worldview of these writers, however, personal experience connected with a larger societal critique.

Many women's novels went beyond social criticism and sought to inspire liberal activism. Not just Harriet Beecher Stowe but Fanny Fern, Lydia Maria Child, Harriet Jacobs, Angelina Grimké, Frances Harper, Pauline Hopkins, Sojourner Truth, and Grace Greenwood addressed abolition, suffrage, and labor reform. Women writers were able to claim a legitimate public presence by arguing that feminine "influence" would temper the inequities of American capitalism. Through women's intervention in the public sphere, American culture would become more humane, more moral, more Christian. Women would usher in the Millennium, a perfect, just, Christian utopia.

A perfect society would come one reader at a time. Women writers were appealing to readers' compassion, loyalty, love of family, and sense of duty to enact a millennial vision of social justice. They depended, financially and artistically, on their relationship with their readers—on the assumption that it was familiar, intimate, and safe. Both readers and writers accepted common stereotypes that seem untenable today: the Christian influence of women, the power of redemption, the misery of sin, and the glory of martyrdom. And yet the emotional resonance of sentimental writing depended on the common acceptance of a Christian worldview, and even rebels like Fanny Fern didn't stray too far.

The paradoxical result was, often, a powerful critique of American society. Sentimental women writers used Christian theology to make emotional appeals that criticized limited government, racial discrimination, and the emerging role of industrial capitalism. Jane Tompkins's famous analysis of *Uncle Tom's Cabin* points to a millennial matriarchy as the logical outcome of this liberal Christian vision—a woman-centered alternative countering the capitalist ethos of American society (144). Indeed, Tompkins argues that "Stowe's very conservatism—her reliance on established patterns of living and traditional beliefs—is precisely what gives her novel its revolutionary potential" (145). The peculiar combination—radicalism through conservatism, social change through individual experience—continues to mark the tradition of activist women's writing.

Sentimental novels fell into critical disfavor during the Gilded Age of the late nineteenth century, as Joan Hedrick notes in her biography of Harriet Beecher Stowe. The *Nation* undercut the cultural power of antebellum women novelists by "attack[ing] the literary excellence of women writers in the name of 'art' " (349). Women's novels have suffered a critical stigma ever since, largely because of their appeal to readers' pleasure and their investment in the marketplace. Jane Tompkins indicted all of twentieth-century literary criticism when she wrote that it has "taught generations of students to equate popularity with debasement, emotionality with ineffectiveness, religiosity with fakery, domesticity with triviality, and all of these, implicitly, with womanly inferiority" (123). These judgments have affected all women writers, but especially the authors of women's novels. The genre survived, though, during the Progressive era.

Progressive Novels: Pragmatist Aesthetics and Women's Writing

Progressivism is the second important critical matrix for this study. By "progressivism" I mean, first, the political and literary activities associated with the Progressive movement at the turn of the century; and second, progressive attitudes toward reform and literature that remained influential, if in modified forms, during the interwar period. The Progressive movement was characterized by a remarkable breadth and range of reform impulse. Progressives advocated for equitable labor laws, prohibition, racial equality, suffrage, abolition, women's rights, public education, trust-busting, and conservation.

All these drives stemmed from an anxiety about the fate of American democracy in an industrial society that seemed increasingly impersonal, corporate, and indifferent. Ironically, the Progressive movement has most often been associated by later observers with that same impersonal bureaucracy. Many historians have indicted Progressivism as an ethos of bureaucratic and corporate management, which replaced local efforts with the centralized control of experts, embedding in its structures elitist and implicitly racist assumptions about the intelligence and abilities of ordinary people. The Progressive movement, other critics charged, used reform to create an atmosphere of "corporate liberalism" that suppressed more revolutionary change.[2] Progressives' faith in experts, their passion for organizing, and their embrace of the corporate model belied their protest and contributed to (in Alan Trachtenberg's phrase) the "incorporation of America."

This book is neither a comprehensive analysis of the Progressive era nor a manifesto on its mixed legacy. I would, however, like to add a footnote to these dismissals of a complex cultural moment. The contradictions of the Progressive movement—its passion for justice, its nativist racism, its creative solutions, its bureaucratic hierarchies—continue to mark activism and liberal politics in the twentieth century. They also mark the careers of Canfield, Fauset, Buck, and Herbst, in the roles they assumed and in their reception.

In this study, I focus on the Progressive era's technologically transformed print culture and on that culture's often complicated relationship with activism. Innovations in printing technology at the turn of the century (and the concomitant increase in advertising) made newspapers and magazines inexpensive, and thus accessible to a much larger audience (Tebbel and Zuckerman 149). *Munsey's, McClure's,* and *The Ladies' Home*

Journal had millions of readers, but scores of more inexpensive magazines had sizable circulations and evolving audiences. American writers had often dreamed of speaking to a national audience, but before the explosion of print technology, the cost of books and "serious" magazines, as well as distribution difficulties, had limited the number of actual readers. At the turn of the century, cheap publishing and an increasing demand for writing made a national audience that cut across geographic, ethnic, and class boundaries seem not only possible but inevitable.

Some writers recoiled. Barbara Hochman argues that nineteenth-century readers regularly "read for the author," feeling the writer's presence as that of a trusted friend (2). Now writers had thousands of instant best friends, some of whom, furthermore, were increasingly invasive in wanting personal information. Books and magazines, in some writers' estimation, had transformed the literate public from a known community of like-minded citizens to a motley array of immigrants and boors. Writers began to keep readers at a distance, both personally and, through the third-person objective voice, formally (4).

Yet not all writers responded with alarm. Some thought that the print revolution was inherently democratic, creating a sustaining public for serious writers (Wilson xiv). Cheap printing, public libraries, and universal education—what cultural critics dismissed as an increasing standardization—would build an ethnically and economically mixed, truly national, culture.

The patron saintof this utopian faith in print was John Dewey. Philosopher, educational reformer, and prominent liberal, Dewey was a looming influence in American culture. He is best known as one of the founders of pragmatism, a philosophy that insists on experimentation and experience to determine both personal behavior and societal reform. He rejected the secure theological cosmology of the nineteenth century, but insisted that a lack of fixed values need not be cause for despair.

Dewey's varied intellectual interests share a common core—a faith in the ability of ordinary people to understand and devise solutions to complicated problems. He also believed that ordinary people could create larger, coherent communities that didn't compromise their individuality. Much of that faith in community depended upon the power of literature to connect and transform individuals. In 1916, Dewey conjectured that reading may "institute a more intimate association between human beings separated thousands of miles from each other than exists between dwellers under the same roof" (*Democracy and Education* 5). Technology had suddenly made this connection possible for more Americans than ever before, and Dewey theorized that the explosion of print would be the foundation of true community and a thriving democracy.

Dewey examined the relationship of art to community and democracy in *Art as Experience,* the foundation of pragmatist aesthetics.[3] Only Western culture, he argues, has separated art from common cultural experience in its aesthetic theory; this reveals the stratified and deleterious nature of industrial society. In other cultures, art is an experience "in which the whole creature is alive and in which he possesses his living through enjoyment" (27); it is distinct in its properties but not essentially different from other sensuous experiences of ordinary people, which, too, are aesthetic in their way.

Dewey's argument concerning art's essential connection to other human responses rests on his definition of experience. This, he argues, results when an "organism" interacts with the environment and is transformed "into participation and communication" (22). Unlike simple sensation, however, experience "has a unity" that "is constituted by a single *quality*" (37). Experience, in other words, requires an aware and thinking subject. Thus, both aesthetic responses and intellectual insights are manifestations of that same consciousness. As Dewey explains, "esthetic cannot be sharply marked off from intellectual experience since that latter must bear an esthetic stamp to be itself complete" (38). The unity of aesthetic and intellectual experience, indeed the unity of all experience, is important because it suggests that the aesthetic is already part of ordinary people's experience, not something that only a superior class can acquire. By identifying it as differing in its medium but not in its essence from any other experience, Dewey made the aesthetic as ubiquitous as print during the Progressive era.

What prevents people from recognizing the aesthetic qualities of their ordinary lives? Dewey argues that the biggest enemies are "the humdrum; slackness of loose ends; submission to convention in practice in intellectual procedure" (40). Ordinary experience tends to numb us to the aesthetic already functioning in our lives. Hence, the importance of art, which is a kind of vicarious experience, focusing our attention with its intensity. "An esthetic experience," Dewey tells us,

> can be crowded into a moment only in the sense that a climax of prior long enduring processes may arrive in an outstanding move-

> ment which so sweeps everything else into it that all else is forgotten. That which distinguishes an experience as esthetic is conversion of resistance and tensions, of excitations that in themselves are temptations to diversion, into a movement toward an inclusive and fulfilling close. (56)

The "conversion" of the humdrum into a meaningful "climax" is the essence of the aesthetic for Dewey. A concentrated artistic experience wakes readers to aesthetic experiences all around them, if they can only pay attention.

Creating such an experience is a collaborative process; both writer and reader are essential. Dewey laments that "we have no word in the English language that unambiguously includes what is signified by the two words 'artistic' and 'esthetic,'" which suggests that the two are distinct, unrelated activities (46). An artist works through the "triad" of "the speaker, the thing said, and the one spoken to"; this triad exists "even when the artist works in solitude" (106). To create, "the artist has to become vicariously the receiving audience" (106). An imagined readership, says Dewey, is essential to the creative process, and anticipating reader responses doesn't corrupt art; in a very real sense, such anticipation enables art.

Nor is the reader passive. "To perceive," Dewey explains, "a beholder must *create* his own experience. . . . Without an act of recreation the object is not perceived as a work of art." (54) Readers become partners rather than parasites or a mindless, menacing mass. Readers and writers create pure experience in the exchange.

At the core of this exchange is emotion. Emotion, Dewey argues, plays a key role in how artists select and shape their material. "In the development of an expressive act," he suggests, "the emotion operates like a magnet drawing to itself appropriate material: appropriate because it has an emotional affinity for the state of mind already moving" (69). Such emotional selection, he argues, "extracts matter from a multitude of objects, numerically and spatially separated, and condenses" them into their essence. "This function" is what "creates the 'universality' of a work of art" (67–68). The role of emotion in the creation of a work of art allows for the emotional experience of the recipient.

The primacy of emotion, however, does not suggest the mindless manipulation that many cultural theorists of the interwar period feared, and that fascist use of popular culture seemed to confirm. Aesthetic emotion,

Dewey argues, does not invalidate individuality, because emotions like fear, elation, and love are not "generic" (67). All emotion is contingent and resides in particular situations for particular people: "Save nominally, there is no such thing as *the* emotion of fear, hate, love. The unique, unduplicated character of experienced events and situations impregnates the emotion that is invoked" (67). In fact, the very specificity of emotion is what gives art its peculiar power. Poets and novelists, in particular, construct "a concrete situation and "permit *it* to evoke emotional response. Instead of a description of an emotion in intellectual and symbolic terms, the artist "does the deed that breeds" the emotion" (67). Emotion, then, binds writer and reader and creates the aesthetic experience.

It may seem counterintuitive, but Dewey's aesthetic theory is intimately connected with both his philosophic theory and his liberalism. Dewey firmly believed in both individual agency and a political community that fosters the welfare of all its citizens; the example of aesthetic experience provided a model for him to believe in both simultaneously without finding them contradictory or mutually exclusive:

> But just as it is the office of art to be unifying, to break through conventional distinctions to the underlying common elements of the experienced world, while developing individuality as the manner of seeing and expressing these elements, so it is the office of art in the individual person, to compose differences, to do away with isolations and conflicts among the elements of our being, to utilize oppositions among them to build a richer personality. (248)

Note the parallelism—art develops the community of our own contradictory consciousnesses into a unified individual personality, and the combination of these individual personalities into a functioning community. Art constructs the perfect community, bringing conflict into unity.

Dewey also believed that an updated "collective liberalism" could perform the same trick for American society (*Liberalism and Social Action* 20). The ideals of liberalism were "the conceptions of a common good as the measure of political organization and policy, of liberty as the most precious trait and very seal of individuality, of the claim of every individual to the full development of his capacities" (24). Such goals could be best reached through the strategic interventions of government. "Liberals today," he writes, believe "that organized society must use its powers to establish the conditions under which the mass of individuals can possess actual as distinct from merely legal liberty" (27). The end goal of "actual liberty" is more important than the means used to achieve them. As we shall see below, this issue reverberated in the debates of the interwar period over book clubs and other corporate efforts to distribute books.

Liberalism, for Dewey, was not just about "liberty of belief and action" but "is associated with a generosity of outlook" (23). Pragmatist aesthetics explained how art could achieve liberal goals. Dewey believed that reading could overcome racial, economic, and gender divides (Hutchinson 47) by providing experience to other cultures and peoples. "Civilization," he explains, "is uncivil because human beings are divided up into non-communicating sects, races, nations, classes and cliques" (*Art as Experience* 336). Reading, then, allows readers not just to communicate with, to have an experience with, but to sympathize with and understand different cultures. Dewey's insistence on this point stemmed from his involvement with Julian Barnes, an eccentric millionaire who turned his Philadelphia Main Line home into a museum of African culture and art. Dewey was also influenced by his lecture tours to Japan and to China; in 1919, he lectured during the rise of New Literature in China, influencing a whole generation of Chinese educators, most notably Hu Shih, the philosopher and educator at Beijing University.

Dewey's faith that art could both make sense of and build community in a multicultural America provided a utopian escape from the often sobering political compromises of American life. Unlike social science, Dewey concludes in *Art as Experience,* "Art is a mode of prediction not found in charts and statistics, and it insinuates possibilities of human relation not to be found in rule and precept, admonition and administration" (349). This could be Dewey's posthumous response to the critics of Progressivism. He was more interested in the possibilities of people, which art epitomized, than in a soulless administration of experts who look only at the greatest good for the greatest number. Dewey's focus was always on the full development of each individual, regardless of race, class, or gender. He clung to the possibility that art could translate such idealistic goals into reality.

This was a faith that many Progressive writers shared. Christopher Morley, an original Book-of-the-Month Club judge, wrote a fascinating parable of middle-class fetishizing of books in his 1919 mystery *The Haunted Bookshop.* Roger Mifflin, the owner of a used-book shop, looks to books as the only salvation for an America reeling from the effects of the Great War. Books, he firmly believes, can construct a world that eliminates the need for war altogether; at present, "printer's ink" is in fierce competition with "gunpowder," but if enough people over enough time depend upon books, the gunpowder can be overcome. Morley's charming farce humorously challenges this middle-class focus on the book and on education. A German pharmacist plans to assassinate the bookish President Wilson on his voyage to Versailles by planting a bomb within the covers of a book. Mifflin foils the plot, but the bomb inadvertently blows up all the books in his bookshop; books, in the end, literally explode. And their explosion preserves Wilson's Progressive mission to save democracy—at least for the time being.

Morley's fable explicitly connects books' revolutionary power to functioning democracy. In their reverence for literature's power, Morley and other Progressive writers were heirs to the Victorian vision of culture as "non-commercial and sacred" (Turner 22). Like their Victorian forebears, they believed that literature contained universal truths that could educate, ennoble, and transform. For politically committed writers, the vicarious experience that literature could provide was the only hope of a democracy threatened by its own size and its ethnic and economic divisions.

Though many of the most prominent writers of the Progressive era were self-consciously virile men (Wilson xiv), this Progressive faith in the power of print had particular appeal for women's novelists. On the surface, of course, pragmatist aesthetics would seem to have little to do with the literary tradition of sentimental reform. Louis Menand argues that pragmatism arose as a protest against this very tradition. Pragmatists like Charles Sanders Peirce, Oliver Wendell Holmes, and William James felt that the horrors of the Civil War had been caused by the rigid, principled self-righteousness of reformers. Through pragmatism, they hoped to arrive at a more flexible, and less destructive, means of determining "right" action.

Pragmatism, however, was entirely consistent with the wave of reform that swept the United States during the Progressive era, as John Dewey's career makes clear. Christian emphasis on the salvation of the individual soul was replaced by a humanist focus on the individual. William James, for example, explicitly rejected Christian notions of absolute truth as the appropriate foundation for action; he claimed that "truth grows up inside of all the finite experiences. They lean on each other, but the whole of them, if such a whole there be, leans on nothing" (260–261). And yet, the ultimate purpose of this contingent reasoning was still linked to absolute, Christian notions of justice; the ultimate purpose of pragmatism was to discover "some of the conditions of the world's deliverance" (284). The actualized self replaced God as the supreme good.

Such Christian overtones and pragmatic methods meant that many women writers could embrace modern philosophy and strategies and yet retain the assumptions of their sentimental foremothers. Dewey's belief in the power of art "to compose differences, to do away with isolations and conflicts among the elements of our being, to utilize oppositions among them to build a richer personality" echoes the belief that "the worth of souls is great in the sight of God." Influenced by the Progressive movement, these writers looked toward a society in which individuals could rise to their full potential without being hindered or crushed by societal restrictions, prejudice, or economic deprivation. It was a distinctly secular form of millennial vision.

Many women writers believed that their fiction contributed to this vision. The belief in the power of fiction to transform society; the emphasis on a symbiotic relationship between writer and reader; the importance of fiction in making the reader "feel right" to overcome prejudice and injustice—these similarities between sentimental women's fiction and Dewey's pragmatist aesthetics suggest an on-going tradition of activist women's fiction.[4] George Hutchinson, in *The Harlem Renaissance in Black and White,* was the first scholar to suggest that pragmatist aesthetics influenced interwar writing, specifically that of the Harlem writers and critics. In this study, I build on Hutchinson's work to argue that pragmatist aesthetics are a crucial tool in understanding politically committed women writers during the same period. Dorothy Canfield and Jessie Fauset came of age during the Progressive era, and their connection to Dewey is strong; Pearl Buck and Josephine Herbst had no direct connection, but their aims as writers can be interpreted usefully through his aesthetic theory. Pragmatist aesthetics connects Progressive era authorship with 1850s women's novels and with middlebrow authorship. All three point toward a similar approach to reading and writing. Progressivism evolves into "progressive" or "liberal" attitudes and undertakings in the interwar period—a focus on individualism and on racial, gender, and economic equity. Subsequent uses of the term "progressive" rely on this general definition.

The Interwar Period: Modernist Aesthetics and Middlebrow

Interwar popular women's novels are just beginning to receive critical attention.[5] Discussions of women writers still tend to be incidental to other concerns: the Harlem Renaissance, radical literature, popular culture, and especially modernism, the dominant paradigm for twentieth-century American writing. A larger critique of modernism is beyond the scope of this book. A brief survey of recent critical work on modernism, however, reveals modernist writers' profound engagement with the literary marketplace.[6] It is curious that, despite the preponderance of evidence, modernist writers—and scholars, like the full professor who snidely commented that "Joyce, Woolf, Ford, et al. were not after all junior academics with a way to make" (Dettmar and Watt 1)—have concocted a fiction of aesthetic and cultural purity, with brave modernist artists confronting a feminized mass culture. Recent scholarship renders many of these distinctions between "commercial" and "artistic" much more difficult to make.

Nor is modernism's formal experimentation innately superior to popular, more conventional forms. Many critics continue to insist that modernism is aesthetically superior because it refuses easy identification and disrupts expectations, thus acting as "a powerful force in *invalidating* the actually prevailing bourgeois values, namely, by shifting the locus of the individual's realization from the domain of the performance principle and the profit motive to that of the inner resources of the human being: passion, imagination, conscience" (Marcuse 4–5; see also Adorno). But estimable scholars have demonstrated that this belief is as mythical as that of modernism's independence from the marketplace. Frederic Jameson, for example, argues that modernist aesthetics were deeply implicated in capitalist culture; Paul Morrison indicts modernism for complicity with reactionary social movements in the twenties and thirties.[7] Formal innovation and progressive politics, such studies show, are not inextricably linked.

Building on this scholarship, *America the Middlebrow* assumes that modernism is a critical construction that cannot account for the entire range of writing and authorship in the interwar period. It has already been stretched to its limit, I would argue, in including women modernists, Harlem Renaissance writers, and proletarian writers. Many other models of authorship can be seen in looking at literature of the interwar period, but these writers have not enjoyed cultural cachet, manifestos, and fifty years of critical work. Yet we can understand more about the range of modern American authorship if we consider these other models worthy of attention.

To examine alternative modes of authorship, I pay particular attention to the details of each writer's career—how she imagined her role as a writer, how she imagined her relationship with readers, and how she negotiated the material conditions of interwar publishing, particularly in relating to agents and publishers and their collective decisions about advertising, book design, and promotion. These details are not superfluous but central to authorship. I also build on the larger scholarship of book history in this emphasis on the material and imaginative conditions of authorship.[8]

One such category of interwar authorship has languished under the term "middlebrow."[9] In common usage, "middlebrow" is an invective that dismisses writing that is neither trash nor art, but somewhere, uncomfortably, in between. Depending on the context, "middlebrow" can mean "middle class," "effeminate," "polluted by commerce," "mediocre," or "sentimental." The term, Janice Radway tells us, emerged in the twenties to describe book clubs and their readers, particularly the Book-of-the-Month Club (*Feeling* 208). Modern critics feared that book clubs were a devolution of the book industry into "conveyor-belt culture" (208). Readers had become so passive that they allowed a group of experts to select their reading for them, instead of relying on their individual taste. Book clubs, through their high-handed "advice" and their intensive marketing and advertising, would corrupt literature, make it just another commodity. Both book-distribution institutions and the readers they served were dismissed with the pejorative "middlebrow," which transformed a demographic—middle-class—into a quality—a blend of mediocrity, greed, and sentimentality.

In interwar diction, "middlebrow" was clearly an insult. In scholarly work, however, more descriptive and nuanced definitions emerge. Rubin defines "middlebrow" by its institutions, focusing on self-education and a nineteenth-century Arnoldian quest for "culture"; Janice Radway defines "middlebrow" by its reading practices, particularly their complicity in twentieth-century capitalism.

Rubin's *The Making of Middlebrow Culture* investigates educational institutions of the twenties and thirties, such as the Book-of-the-Month Club, the radio show *Information Please,* and Will Durant's accessible history, *The Story of Philosophy;* her study combines historical overviews with biographical and literary readings. For Rubin, these institutions extend nineteenth-century genteel culture, which taught that the "universal" values of literature could inoculate the masses against materialism and radicalism. Many middlebrow critics worked or had been trained as teachers, but wanted to reach a wider audience, bypassing classroom education for entrepreneurial ventures. They established themselves as a new class of mediators between readers and cultural capital, with a complicated relationship to cultural authority.

Middlebrow critics, Rubin argues, resisted American culture's larger shift from "character" to a more superficial "personality" under the influence of capitalism. Yet because they were embracing the institutions of market capitalism—the very catalyst for that transformation—their attempts were ultimately futile. Rubin faults middlebrow critics for their aesthetic choices as well. "When middlebrow popularizers accommodated consumer priorities," she writes, "worthwhile aesthetic commitments were also lost in the bargain" (xix).

Radway, by contrast, faults middlebrow culture not for its aesthetic inferiority, but for its status-quo apoliticism. *A Feeling for Books* focuses on middlebrow reading practices through a cultural history of the Book-of-the-Month Club (BOMC). This, Radway argues, was a quintessentially twentieth-century institution; unlike genteel cultural guardians, the BOMC embraced the book as a commodity, wedding literature to circulation, advertising, and profit. It catered to the needs of middlebrow readers, who sought intense emotional response instead of a disinterested appreciation of formal qualities. Middlebrow readers were defined primarily as consumers, participating in a frankly entrepreneurial venture.

Middlebrow readers' emotional response, in Radway's view, was no less implicated in capitalism than their club membership. "Middlebrow organizations such as the Book-of-the-Month Club," she contends, "helped acclimate us to the business of consumer culture and ushered us into a particular life world still too complacent about certain social hierarchies" (12). The intense emotion awakened by the middlebrow served only to placate the middle class in their sterile lives under capitalism; it created for the middle class a kind of "dream world," which avoided potentially upsetting or challenging topics like race. "Too often," she concludes, the solution to "serious social problems" was the "moral, ethical, and spiritual rehabilitation of the individual subject alone" (13). This focus on individual transformation is an accurate depiction of the mode of domestic political fiction I have been tracing. Radway's conclusion that this focus on the individual is an apolitical "personalism," however, misses the political connections many writers built on such individual appeals.

These two complaints—aesthetic inferiority and political obtuseness—recur in most critical discussions of middlebrow culture. Not coincidentally, I believe, both Rubin and Radway view this as primarily passive, focusing on distribution and reception. Middlebrow culture, both assume, acts upon readers through capitalist institutions. Neither writer considers the possibility that middlebrow writing is created by design, not by default.

This book is interested primarily in neither middlebrow institutions nor middlebrow readers but in middlebrow *authorship*. While theories about the political orientation of the middle class and its reading practices intersect with the question of authorship, I am more interested in how writers imagined their reading audience than in the actual makeup of the audience, which scholars like Rubin and Radway have discussed in depth. I am also less interested in a critique of the "middle class" or "middle-class values," though some of these assumptions about readers make their way into how the writers I examine understood their audience. Middlebrow writers define their sense of authorship by what they imagine their readership to be—not necessarily what that readership really is. I question critical assumptions about middlebrow's aesthetic inferiority and reactionary politics, and instead explore Tad Friend's intriguing premise that there is an "art of the middlebrow," created intentionally (24).

Middlebrow authorship is a posthumous designation. There was no self-identified school of "middlebrow authorship" in the twenties and thirties—no manifestos, no proud articulation of principles. As Trysh Travis wryly notes, no writer aspired to be called "middlebrow" (358). I am constructing a category of authorship that the authors in question likely would have disavowed.

Yet "middlebrow authorship" makes visible some striking continuities between writing of the interwar period, 1850s women's novels, and pragmatist aesthetics. One is in the expectations of readers—expectations that middlebrow authors wrote to satisfy. Elizabeth Long emphasizes several key characteristics of middlebrow reading: identification (606), a strong voice (605–606), character and plot development over formal innovation (606). Identification, an emphasis on character and plot, and formal choices that don't alienate—these emerge as common requirements for middle-class readers, just as they did for sentimental women's novelists and for John Dewey.

Many writers worked consciously to fulfill these readerly desires. Middlebrow authors assume a sympathetic communion between reader and writer; the text offers vicarious experience, understanding, and wisdom. This primary emphasis drove many professional and aesthetic decisions of middlebrow writers, from choice of publisher to choice of genre and form, and it led some middlebrow writers to disavow, deliberately, the cultural capital of "serious" authorship.

Both men and women writers were dismissed as middlebrow during the interwar period; Gordon Hutner has done extensive work on male middlebrow writers of the period,[10] but much more remains to be done. Writing was, however, a cultural activity that was regarded as feminine. Twenties' critics of consumer culture, Radway tells us, describe machines that "appeared to be the result of some natural, organic, fertile force run wild" ("On the Gender" 879), a "Big Mother" that "overwhelmed or smothered distinct, singular, always male individuals" (879). Antimiddlebrow critics contrasted a feminized, amorphous mass with an implicitly male "independent, self-regulating adult" who was essential for democracy (Radway, *Feeling* 227). The implicit gendering of middlebrow writing is another connection with women's activist writing traditions in the 1850s and in the Progressive era.

Radway suggests that antimiddlebrow critics feminized "the new forces of production" to promote "the convenient and encouraging illusion that those forces and the kinds of subjects they called into being might be as easily contained and controlled as women were in a society where men traditionally controlled both the pen and the law" (217). In the 1920s, of course, women were hardly easily contained and controlled. The passage of the Nineteenth Amendment made the twenties and thirties a time of unprecedented political influence for women, as seen in the appointment of the first woman cabinet secretary, Frances Perkins, and in Eleanor Roosevelt's unprecedented visibility and political influence as first lady. Women's new political agency made the political possibilities of middlebrow authorship particularly important for them. The influence of women writers on women readers could have a direct effect on social policy and on government.

In the interwar period, then, a significant number of women writers continued to combine their activism and literary production in what would come to be dismissed as "middlebrow" writing. Not all middlebrow writers were liberal activists, of course. There were some, male and female, whose politics were not progressive, those whose work more supports Radway's characterization of the middlebrow as an opiate for the professional class. Middlebrow authorship is not inherently a progressive undertaking, any more than it is inherently conservative. I argue, however, that a progressive strand of women's middlebrow authorship thrived in the interwar period.

Their combination of activism and middlebrow came through an emphasis on emotion. Middlebrow writers appealed to their readers' positive emotions, or what the modern authors would term sentimental emotions—pity, love, patriotism, self-sacrifice, devotion. They focused their craft on creating the style, plot, characters, and themes that would satisfy the desires of their middle-class audience—not only for characters with whom to identify, but for narratives that would help them to understand modern life. Choices about form and plot had to be made with middlebrow readers in mind—not just their desire for identification, but which situations, characters, and formal choices would foster identification, rather than alienate them. Formal decisions were therefore pragmatic; authors would use any means necessary to move their readers. They adapted tested devices and genres—particularly the romance—to their own purposes, often mixing them.

Much of the activist middlebrow writers' emotional power came from an appropriation of American iconography. Middlebrow writing's embodiment of ill-defined American values, as I discuss in my afterword, was a frequent lament of the first generation of American Studies scholars. Dwight Macdonald, for example, complained that "there is something damnably American about the middlebrow" (59). Indeed, Jennifer Parchesky argues that the very notion of "middle America" was a creation of middlebrow culture during the interwar period. Film and novels, she argues, offered melodramas of everyday life, creating "structures of feeling" that hearkened back to older patterns of middle-class life, before the proprietors of small businesses had given way to salaried white-collar laborers. Parchesky argues that middlebrow writers thus created points of identification for middle-class readers; the "middle America" they created, though, was white and middle-class, a group that was far from making up the majority of Americans, then and now.

That emerging hegemony of "typical American-ness" was a potent source for activist writers. The idea of America—its equality, independence, individualism, freedom—continued to have enormous resonance in the twenties and thirties, despite, or perhaps because of, the enormous changes American society had gone through. It was, despite Jefferson's fervent wish, no longer an agrarian nation, nor was it, as de Crevecoeur had suggested, a friendly conglomeration of western European immigrants. With the end of "free land" in the West (or at least, of the belief that there was free land to be had in the West), the majority of Americans for the first time lived in cities, and a majority worked as wage earners for others, not as independent farmers or small-business owners. Many Marxist critics argue that these economic and societal changes had fundamentally transformed art, exposing the Western tradition as a bourgeois mouthpiece. Frederic Jameson, for example, claims that the rise of industrial capitalism eradicated the traditional notions of art that Dewey advocates in his pragmatist aesthetic; the life stories of individuals couldn't articulate the life of the larger community, as they could in simpler, agrarian cultures.

And yet, none of these changes diminished the emotional resonance that American iconography had for its middle-class readers. If anything, it increased its power, tinged as it was with nostalgia for the past, for an America under assault. The writers I study here sought to transform still potent symbols of the American national into icons of progressivism.

Such mythmaking could backfire, as Jennifer Parchesky's study of interwar middlebrow books and film suggests. Yet "middle America" could be appropriated. Middlebrow writers, black and white, radical and liberal, extended a tradition of appropriation in the interwar period, creating vicarious experiences for their readers,encouraging them to embrace explicitly liberal commitments and political aims. Canfield, Fauset, Buck, and Herbst illustrate the range of this kind of interwar writing.

ONE

Progressive Middlebrow

Dorothy Canfield, Reform, and Women's Magazines

In 1902, before each became a best-selling novelist, Dorothy Canfield and Willa Cather suffered a catastrophic break in their friendship. Cather, preparing her first collection of short stories, *The Troll Garden,* included one called "The Profile," based on Evelyn Osbourne, with whom Canfield and Cather had traveled in Europe. When Canfield read the story, she was concerned that publication would upset Evelyn, and wrote Cather an emotional plea:

> I have read the story and just as you thought I do ask that you do not publish it—not for my own sake but so that you will not have done a cruel thing. . . . I beg you will all my heart . . . not to strike a cruel and overwhelming blow to one who has not deserved it, who has already lost her life's happiness through her deformity, and who was kind to you. . . . Believe me, who have thought with such sick intensity about it that it will injure you in the end—in every way—and I think it would crush Evelyn—I don't believe she would ever recover from the blow of your description of her affliction. (Madigan 26–27)

Canfield's response may seem overly sensitive, and one could read her as choosing personal relationships over art. For Canfield, however, writing was a profoundly human endeavor, an activity whose primary mission was to create an emotional experience for the reader. She could only see Cather's story as a betrayal, not only of friendship but of the calling of authorship as she understood it.

Cather, and her companion Isabelle McClung, writing on her behalf, saw things very differently. The story was Cather's artistic creation, and any connection to a living person was incidental and in the end unimportant. For McClung, the difficult process of artistic work mattered more than the emotional effects the story might have on readers, or one reader in particular. In the end, Canfield felt that her obligation to protect her helpless friend from harm was more important than Cather's right to publish the story. She finally appealed directly to *McClure's*, threatening legal action unless they removed the story, and succeeded in blocking its publication.[1]

Canfield's confrontation with Cather prefigures the writer she would become—a beloved popular novelist who focused, primarily, on the emotional experience of her readers, and was interested in formal technique only as it served that end. Her sympathy toward middle-class readers made modernist critics dismiss her as the great genteel defender.[2] For most of them, Canfield seemed the embodiment of all that kept America from having a "usable past"— the quintessential New England reformer. She consciously constructed her authorial identity with readers, not critics, in mind, and kept doggedly to her political and aesthetic commitments, disregarding cultural capital. Canfield's primary authorial focus on emotion and liberal causes made her a prototypic middlebrow author.

New England Reformer, Redux: Construction of Authorship

Dorothy Canfield was a tireless activist. She introduced Progressive-era readers to Maria Montessori, served on the state board of education, was a Book-of-the-Month Club judge, did relief work in France during World War I, and advocated for the United Nations and universal human rights—this in addition to writing extensive articles, short stories, and novels. Such was her energy that the critic Grant Overton, in 1928, felt the need to lecture her to choose between art and life; he predicted a successful career "if the world can contrive to run itself for a little while" (73).

For Canfield, as for John Dewey, art and life were intertwined; her activism and her writing were complementary activities. The great-granddaughter of abolitionists, with Vermont roots that predated the

Revolutionary War, Canfield was the secular, modern heir of sentimental activist-writers like Harriet Beecher Stowe and Lydia Maria Child. Her father, James Hulme Canfield, a university professor and president, was an advocate of suffrage, civil rights for African Americans, and free trade; her mother, Flavia Canfield, would-be artist, led her daughter on extended stays in Paris and Spain (Washington 16), and introduced her to music, painting, and literature. Canfield was trained thoroughly in the European literary tradition, attending French schools and later the Sorbonne, and earning a Ph.D. in French at Columbia in 1903.

When James Canfield, a college president in Kansas, Nebraska, and Ohio, went to Columbia University to become a librarian, and Canfield enrolled as a graduate student, she became immersed in the muckraking, impassioned, noncomformist atmosphere of Manhattan, She refused to wear a corset and hotly debated free love, atheism, women's rights, racial equality, labor laws, political corruption, economic monopolies, and public education (Yates 70). Exposure to some of the most influential thinkers of the Progressive era, including Franz Boas as well as Dewey, influenced her development as a writer.

Boas, the founder of Columbia's anthropology department, assaulted nineteenth-century scientific racism; his department was at the center of a liberal argument for what we now term "multiculturalism." Racist rhetoric was rampant in America from the 1880s on, with particular venom directed at the threat the "alien" influences of "Negroes" and immigrants posed. By contrast, Boas's idea of race as a cultural, rather than an essential, category helped to establish "America" as the interrelation, with all its creative tension, of all its various peoples, not simply "Anglo-Saxon." One can see Boas's influence in much of Canfield's early writing.[3] She makes a strong fictional argument for America as a truly multicultural place, in desperate need of the talents, perspectives, and culture of all of its citizens, including middle-class white women, immigrants, and African Americans.

Of course, the notion of "culture" cuts both ways; what would have been seen as racist essentialism can be restated in the same terms, as a defense of unique cultures. Julia Ehrhardt has criticized Canfield's involvement in the thirties' eugenics movement, in defense of Vermont Anglo-Saxon "culture" (78). Race is an extremely complicated issue in Canfield's career; she often reflects prejudice against African Americans and Jews, yet she supported legal and social equality, a stance that, ironically, may have helped her persuade an audience that had clung to similar stereotypes.

Canfield's embrace of "culture" was further complicated by her profound distaste for groupthink. Boas provided a sometimes useful understanding of groups, but he did not really alter Canfield's insistence on individualism. She spoke up for groups of people only when cultural prejudices prevented others from seeing their members as individuals. Her *Vermont Tradition: Biography of an Outlook on Life* articulates a utopian ideal of a community of individuals, none of whom impose their values or expectations on anyone else; collective intervention and action are undertaken only to protect the individual's autonomy—in education, for example. Yet she recognized that America had simply gotten too big, too socially stratified, too incorporated for the old "town meeting" ideal of democracy to work. In her antifascist 1939 novel, *Seasoned Timber,* Canfield calls "managing large numbers without affronting human dignity" the challenge of the century, for "the older decent ways of organizing life just crumple up under the weight of modern crowds" (223, 224). What is needed, she suggests, is someone "seriously trying to invent new and decent ways to keep order" (223) that don't depend on violence. The programs of the Progressive era, and later of the New Deal, seemed to satisfy this need.

John Dewey was another important influence on Canfield. His focus on education, his insistence on contingent truth and pragmatic results, and his theory of art as pure experience had an enormous impact on Canfield's subsequent career as a popular novelist and public intellectual. Canfield was the first American to write about Maria Montessori and to advocate her teaching method, one that rivaled Dewey's. She believed, as Dewey did, in the importance of education in creating true democracy and a cohesive community. Her later book on adult education for the Carnegie Foundation, *Why Stop Learning?,* her participation on the Vermont board of education, and her work on the Book-of-the-Month Club all stemmed from a Deweyan commitment to democratic education. Robert Frost, in fact, claimed that Canfield had turned Vermont into a "welfare state." She responded "that the Puritan word 'Commonwealth' meant exactly the same thing" (Frost).

Like Dewey, Canfield believed that reading was the foundation of a functioning democracy. The process of reading itself, she explained, promotes intellectual maturity, because through reading "responsible books filled with the qualifications, the careful accuracies, the rounded views inconceivable to the fifteen-minute snippets of the radio," a reader develops the "mental discipline . . . necessary before forming an opinion" ("Book Clubs"). Reading educates citizens to reject totalitarianism and embrace democracy.

Canfield went further in defining the kind of emotion such vicarious experience provided. For her, the core of aesthetic experience was an inspired moment of human sympathy. The craft of writing, for Canfield, encouraged readers to experience another perspective. Years after she began her writing career—at a lecture at Yale in 1928, and in the preface to her 1947 retrospective collection of essays, *A Harvest of Stories*—Canfield articulated her aesthetic of sympathy and vicarious experience. Both center on her first "aesthetic" experience as a child in Paris, one that biographer Ida Washington claims would fix her definition of the literary for the rest of her life (49). Waiting for her mother in a museum, Canfield saw a painting of a dwarf, Sebastian DeMorra:

> Above his dwarfed body, there looked out a full-grown man's face, terrible in its quiet sadness. I could not pass along that wall without stopping to meet his darkly shadowed eyes. It was as if he had a wordless message for me, a compelling one. In the end even the hard, adolescent crust over my shallow, undeveloped heart was pierced with an involuntary, persistent compassion for human ills, which has been for me, as for everybody who admits that skeleton into his inner closet, a disquieting cause for heavy-heartedness. (*The Bedquilt* xx)

Canfield's language demonstrates her ideal aesthetic, which can compel involuntary, persistent sympathy in even the most "shallow, undeveloped heart." The painting "pierces" her, causing an experience of intense sympathy and communion, despite its subject's off-putting exterior. For her mother, art was a refuge from the degradations of ordinary life; for Canfield, though, it ennobled ordinary experience by making it not only understandable but also inspiring. The "tragedy of the dwarf man," she wrote, "opened my heart to share the sorrow of the victims of modern man's ignorant inability to mend flaws in the social structure and standards" (xxvii). Much of the suffering of ordinary people, she believed, derived from an outmoded and inadequate "social structure," and she embedded critiques of such structures in her fiction.

Her first short story, "The Bedquilt," was an appreciative discussion of an old maid who wins an award at the local fair for her quilting. Aunt Mehetabel "was as helplessly starved as the Spanish dwarf of what all human beings need for growth . . . was as humbled before her fellow-men through no fault of hers . . . as defenselessly given over to the careless mockery of those luckier than she" (xxvii). Because she was plain, unmarried and poor, she was unthinkingly mocked. Canfield would appreciate her dignity, her innately interesting life, having had that encounter with a painting, which brought back "the patient remembered eyes of an insignificant old maid whom I had known in my careless childhood" (xxvii). These two moments of painful sympathy led her to a life of fiction, which Canfield described not as rebellious, superior, or distinguishing but as "the heartsick turmoil of a compulsion to imagine and desperately to try to portray a human being not as what she seemed, but what she was . . . to convince people who in life hardly even noticed her existence that she shared in the human dignity of the instinct to create" (xxvii).

For Canfield, fiction brought a sympathetic appreciation of those who have been dismissed and devalued. The tragedy is that we don't understand that, as Dewey insisted, every person has an innate "instinct to create." To see people "as they are" is to see them as unique, important, and creative.

How, then, does a writer's creativity differ from ordinary people's aesthetic experience? Canfield argued that artistic creation comes from moments of "heightened awareness," a "condition of unusual sensitivity by noticing more the things which happen around him," beauty, or injustice, or even just sensory images (Madigan *Keeping Fires* 244). When ordinary people experience such moments, Canfield argues, they don't "make use of it in any way" (244); the writer, though, "knows that his material and the impulse to creative work comes through that particular state of sensitivity" (244). The difference is only of degree and intention:

> The non-writing person accepts that new understanding and incorporates it with his own personal life. The impulse of the writing person is to share this new understanding with the rest of humanity. He feels its importance as a help to understanding what takes place

> around us, and can hardly wait until he has put it into some form in which, he hopes, others may see the significance of events in human life which they have been taking perhaps callously, perhaps just with dull or slow lack of understanding.
>
> What had come to me, there in the Norwegian garden, was a vision of the universality of sensitiveness among all human beings. (Madigan *Keeping Fires* 244)

The universality of sensitiveness was at the center of Canfield's aesthetic, and would remain there over the course of her career. The aesthetic experience, then, was a heightened experience of *ordinary* people, not something set apart for the enlightened. She wrote in 1927 that "all we consider great in art, or in intelligence or in wise living, owes its greatness to its expression of ideals common to all human beings *in their highest moments" (Why Stop Learning?* 149). In fact, she argues, "the people" are often savvier about great art than their more cultured contemporaries. "Who supported Shakespeare by steady love and admiration?" she asks. "Not the refined, cultivated elite of his age, but the rabble who crowded into his theater. Who built the Gothic Cathedrals? Not the few delicate-minded poets and litterateurs, but masses and crowds of ordinary folks" (77). This explains Canfield's modest claims about herself as an artist. What made her a writer didn't separate her from common people; it made her, in a sense, the spokesperson for humanity.

Canfield's modesty belied her sophisticated approach to her audience. The critic Elizabeth Wyckoff noted: "It is difficult to separate the literary craftsman in her work from what there is no better word for than the propagandist—a fluent and creative propagandist, to be sure, but always advancing some immensely interesting, adventurous or courageous way to live" (40). Always earnest, always engaging what she saw as "the big questions," Canfield sought to persuade her middle-class audience to more democratic and ideally American behavior.

Her means of persuasion, as her conception of art suggests, was emotion. Carefully preparing her readers to identify with her characters, she bound them to her political and humanistic aims. She denied that the use of emotion was necessarily "sentimental." About a potential Book-of-the-Month Club choice, she wrote "I don't think it is sentimental. By definition, sentimentalism is emotion indulged in for its own sake, beyond what would be natural under the circumstances. The Kantor book seems to me full of real emotion, entirely sincere—and not only natural but inevitable to anyone with a heart in the situation described in the story" (Letter to Harry Scherman 1931). Emotion is not an embarrassment, in her worldview, but a guide and a unifying force—shared emotion reveals what is "natural" to people.

That her writing evoked strong emotions is strikingly apparent from the large file of reader letters in her collected papers, which Jennifer Parchesky discusses at length. Coming from towns small and large all over the country, they are dominated by those from women who consider her a teacher, a prophet, and a friend. The cumulative effect is moving; these women are embarrassed to be writing fan letters, yet want to describe what an impact Canfield's novels have had on them. "I have always known I like your writing," says Peggy Davis. "There is solidity and firmness there—though I've noticed that you can make tangible half-spoken and 'unclear' emotions and thoughts that someone else would disregard entirely. That's the next thing I like so tremendously—your understanding" (Davis Letter to Canfield). Other letters echo Davis's comment—that Canfield both articulates her readers' feelings and ideas and helps to guide them toward more meaningful lives. One writer from Cincinnati compares Canfield's novels to the Bible; another notes "the feeling of uplift and delight that I have felt at the conclusion of each story"; a third thanks her for "supply[ing] people, not with ready-made nightmares, but with some encouragement and help in this business of living" (Widle Letter to Canfield; Desbecker Letter to Canfield; Mills Letter to Canfield). And readers thank her for writing in language that doesn't demean or mystify them. One appreciates the fact that in Canfield's novels, "the problems of technique . . . are buried out of sight, like a clean-swept house only whose ordered loveliness is proof of earlier labors, as they should be," for because of this, "I *lived* in your book. In the reality of it, I couldn't stop to think 'But how beautifully this is done!'—and that, it seems to me, is a major tribute" (Van Slyke Letter to Canfield). No statement more succinctly describes the desired effect of Canfield's aesthetic; the author's labor results in seeming transparency, an accessibility that allows for absolute identification with characters and the implicit worldview. Canfield provides a reading experience that educates without belittling, advocates without berating.

As is evident from her description of the composition of "The Bedquilt," issues of gender were central to Canfield's aesthetic. She didn't perceive herself as a traditional feminist, advocating for suffrage as her father had. She did, however, insist on the dignity and humanity of ordinary middle-class women. Modern vilification of the "Victorian matriarch" was as nonsensical as glorification of her. In her 1927 *Why Stop Learning?*, she discusses the moderns' hostility to middle-class women and their educational clubs. The reason, Canfield explains,

> is that same old hostility to more widespread enlightenment we have already seen existing in the mind of a certain kind of cultivated person, the traditional feeling that "culture" is the sacred emblem of the tribe, shown only to those few initiates who have learned the secret passwords which let them into the culture-chief's lodge. It is to be remembered that among primitive people, the secret and sacred tribal emblem is never shown to women. (88)

In her astute analysis of highbrow's fetishizing of culture, Canfield repudiates modernist misogyny. Cultural elitism is an unacceptable anachronism.

Highbrows, she says, "feel the same intimate distaste for the idea of education open to every one which their grandfathers felt for the idea of the alphabet open to every one. They feel it the same sort of penetrating blow struck at their superiority. And they are right. It is" (16). She grants that conservatives may be right who claim that if "attention is paid to the taste of the general public . . . the ruling taste will become bad" (70), but she prefers "the faithful lovers and friends of ordinary people who have a mystic faith in their possibilities as the best hope for us all. . . . [They] are fighting for the privilege of flinging open to all the world the doors of the storehouse of civilization's experience and aspirations" (77). To succeed in mass education, one must neither "give the public what it wants" nor "try to force it to take what you think it ought to have" (148), but, "as usual . . . steer a middle course":

> [You] must give up some of the fine flowers and bloom of culture you think people ought to have but apparently do not want; you must patiently consider ways and means to emphasize what is good in what they already want; above all, you must invent means to bring out their unguessed latent desire for better things. This is not a base compromise with ugly reality; it is only common sense applied to

> education. It is not base, because all normal, unperverted, reasonably healthy human beings do honestly desire something better than what they have. All they need from a teacher is to be reminded of that desire, to be shown how to try to attain it instead of stifling or mutilating or caricaturing this instinctive human reach upwards. (148)

Canfield's assumptions betray a faith in ordinary people's goodness and potential that rivals Christian faith in their eternal souls. Assuming that "normal, unperverted, reasonably healthy human beings" have universal needs, of course, could allow anyone who doesn't share these desires to be labeled as perverted and abnormal. Yet Canfield is less interested in demonizing the marginal than in understanding the mainstream, and promotes a "middle course" that respects her readers, while working to persuade them to what she saw as a better way.

Negotiation of the Marketplace, 1900–1940

That middle course developed for Canfield as a magazine writer in the Progressive era. She had the good fortune to be contacted by Paul R. Reynolds, one of the first literary agents in America. Though agents would become commonplace in the twenties, they were still somewhat rare in the first decade of the twentieth century. Reynolds offered his services to Canfield; she was skeptical that his 10 percent fee could be justified in higher sales. They decided to begin on a trial basis (Madigan *Keeping Fires* 39). Reynolds used his formidable knowledge to place more of Canfield's stories, at higher fees, than she had ever managed to.

The relationship went beyond a lucrative professional partnership, however; Reynolds was a friend, an adviser, and a trusted critic. Canfield asked his advice about article topics before she wrote them, to be sure that the essay would sell. He offered suggestions about titles, plot, and structure (Reynolds Letter to Canfield 15 January 1932). He also discussed selling strategies, smoothed over conflicts with editors, and encouraged her to accommodate the marketplace in dealing with magazines while keeping her integrity intact in her books (Reynolds Letter to Canfield 9 February 1930). Reynolds saw himself as a man of letters as well as a businessman; in his correspondence with Canfield, he is as interested in plot and style as he is in marketability.

Warm as Canfield's relationship with her agent was, it was surpassed by that with her editor. Canfield first met Alfred Harcourt at one of her parents' Sunday afternoon teas when he was a student at Columbia; he was the roommate of Canfield's soon-to-be husband John Fisher (Harcourt *Some Experiences* 23). Canfield had no way of knowing how esteemed a career Harcourt would have in publishing. He worked first as a salesman and then as an editor at Henry Holt, where he handled Canfield's writing, as well as that of respected figures like Robert Frost and Sinclair Lewis.

In 1919, Harcourt got into a dispute with Henry Holt over the publication of a book by Bertrand Russell. Frustrated with Holt's conservative approach, he decided to start his own firm (30–31). Fortune smiled on it from the beginning. Sinclair Lewis and Canfield went over to him, and started the twenties with a literary feud that resulted in both topping the best-seller list in 1921 (58). Harcourt gave Canfield the attention due a best-selling writer. Harcourt, Brace and Company, incidentally, was one of the few firms in New York to pay and promote women equally; this probably was due to the influence that Harcourt's second wife, Ellen, had in the formation of the company (Tebbel *A History* 133).

Canfield trusted Harcourt as an editor, deferring to him in business matters and accepting title and editorial suggestions. Harcourt may have been the model for Vincent Marsh, the love interest at the center of her first true best seller, *The Brimming Cup*. The professional relationship of John Fisher, Alfred Harcourt, and Dorothy Canfield remained strong, however. Harcourt continued to publish and promote Canfield's writing, and told her in 1933, "this perhaps is an occasion when I may say that the business and personal relations that have developed between us in all these years have meant probably more to me than anything else I got out of publishing" (Letter to Canfield 13 June 1933).

Canfield, then, had all the conditions required for literary success—leisure to write, sympathetic and well-paying periodicals, a skilled and aggressive agent, a prestigious and financially solvent publishing house. World War I brought her fame. She and her family traveled to France before the United States entered the war. John Fisher, true to his Quaker background, drove ambulances; Canfield did relief work and wrote short stories. Her war writing focused not on battles but on the effect of the war on ordinary people—doctors, farmers, pharmacists, teachers. It may have promoted stories of German atrocities and served as propaganda for the virtuous, victimized French allies, as critics charged; it also refused to make war the main intention of human beings.

Canfield became a celebrity when the United States entered the war, and her writing was desperately sought by mainstream magazines. Afterwards, when general disillusionment with the outcome of the war led to a rejection of Progressivism and liberal politics, her relationships with many of those same magazines were severed. In 1920 *Everybody's* rejected her proposed novel, *The Brimming Cup.* What could have been a disaster became her greatest success, however, through the postwar rise of women's magazines.

In the twenties, women's magazines purchased women's writing at unheard-of prices. *Everybody's* had paid $3,000 for the serialization rights to *The Squirrel Cage* in 1910; *McCall's,* outbidding *Woman's Home Companion,* paid $15,000 sight unseen for *The Brimming Cup* in 1920, a figure that Canfield, writing confidentially to her agent Paul Reynolds, thought "a perfectly sinfully whopping price" (Letter to Reynolds 12 February 1920). And prices would go up throughout the twenties and early thirties. *Woman's Home Companion* bought her novels for $20,000 to serialize them and in 1933, at the height of the Depression, paid $30,000 for the serialization rights to *Bonfire* (Reynolds 17–18).

Woman's Home Companion provided more than money, however; its savvy editor, Gertrude Lane, created a reading community uniquely suited to Canfield's aesthetic and progressive commitments. Lane was the editor of the magazine from 1911 until 1941, and she presented a welcome alternative to the patronizing attitude of male editors like Edward Bok at the *Ladies' Home Journal.*[4] Lane was a self-made woman, rising from an entry-level position to that of editor-in-chief, earning $50,000 a year (Tebbel and Zuckerman 99). She was also the vice president of the Crowell Corporation, the only woman in the upper echelons of management (Thornton Academy Distinguished Alumni). Lane improved the circulation of her magazine to three million a year, making the *Woman's Home Companion* the most-read women's magazine of the twenties and thirties.

In promotional material, Lane articulated her philosophy of the magazine:

> In editing the *Woman's Home Companion,* I keep constantly in mind a picture of the housewife of today as I see her. She is not the woman who wants to do *more* housework, but the woman who wants to do *less* housework so that she will have more time for other things. She is intelligent and clearheaded. I must tell her the truth. She is busy;

> I must not waste her time. She is forever seeking new ideas; I must keep her in touch with the best. Her horizon is ever extending, her interests broadening, the pages of the *Woman's Home Companion* must reflect the sanest and most constructive thought on the vital issues of the day. (Tebbel and Zuckerman 99)

Lane clearly regarded housewives not as drudges or conspicuous consumers but as important individuals. In this, she disagreed with many women's magazine editors and with the rhetoric about the Victorian matriarch that dominated so many "modern" magazines. As John Tebbel and Mary Ellen Zuckerman explain, Lane believed "that women were thinking, sensitive human beings with many interests outside the home" (99).

Gertrude Lane also incorporated an unusual emphasis on politics, particularly Progressive politics, into her magazine. She encouraged middle-class women to be politically active citizens. After the ratification of the Nineteenth Amendment in 1920, many women's magazines shifted part of their focus toward educating women to more active participation in political and public life. The *Woman's Home Companion,* for example, had a regular column for "new voters," and published articles that encouraged women to run for office and organize for causes like increased school funding. Some of the leading political writers of the day contributed articles and brief biographies to women's magazines, and presidential candidates frequently took out full-page advertisements, as did the Republican Warren G. Harding in a 1924 issue of *McCall's.* The *Woman's Home Companion* proudly detailed its commitment to women in politics in a preelection editorial in 1924, and had long supported woman suffrage, even as the *Ladies' Home Journal,* edited by Edward Bok, opposed it. Gertrude Lane updated nineteenth-century republican motherhood for a changed social scene that now allowed direct political involvement. The *Woman's Home Companion* may have justified women's political involvement through their noble influence as mothers; it was also, nevertheless, encouraging overt political expression.

The *Woman's Home Companion* was also, not coincidentally, a leading publisher of fiction in the twenties and thirties. It was an ideal forum for popular women writers like Edna Ferber, Fannie Hurst, Kathleen Norris, Willa Cather, Pearl Buck, and Ellen Glasgow; it also published men like Sinclair Lewis, F. Scott Fitzgerald, and Sherwood Anderson. For Dorothy

Canfield, the magazine provided a direct connection with the middlebrow women readers she focused on.

Canfield's first women's magazine publication in the twenties, though, appeared not in *Woman's Home Companion* but in *McCall's,* where she entered into public debate as the opponent of modern cynicism and rejection of middle-class life.

"The Other Side of Main Street": *The Brimming Cup*

The publication history of *The Brimming Cup,* serialized in 1920 and published in book form in 1921, provides a striking example of Canfield's political influence through her writing in women's magazines. The period of the bohemian twenties is often said to have begun with the publication of a novel that became a runaway best seller and the topic of spirited discussion and debate: Sinclair Lewis's *Main Street.* Known as the book that "shattered one of the most sacred American myths, that of the friendly village" (Hutchisson 9), *Main Street* sparked a "national debate" about American materialism, hypocrisy, conservatism, class hierarchy, and indifference to art and beauty. The novel details Carol Kennicott's hopeless attempt to combat the mind-numbing banality of her small town. Her failure to overcome or even resist the mediocrity of small-town America, which was traditionally seen as the bulwark of democracy, exposes the bankruptcy of American civilization and justifies modern revolt against cultural mores. For Lewis, to understand the common man in America was to despise him. The publication of *Main Street* threw down a gauntlet, dividing Americans into the worthy and the inane.

James Hutchisson explains the larger cultural effect of Lewis's novel: "Editorials debated its veracity, a popular song entitled "Main Street" appeared, and parodies of the story followed" (43). The term "Main Street" became part of the vernacular (as "Babbitt" would later). Another less-noted aspect of the novel is its rejection of political activism. *Main Street* is as much a critique of the reform tradition as a "revolt from the village." Lewis satirizes Carol Kennicott, a nascent reformer, as relentlessly as he does the boors of Gopher Prairie. She wants to transform the town into a place of beauty and grace, a dream the prosaic Dr. Kennicott shamelessly manipulates. The middle class, hostile to culture, refinement, and beauty, vehemently opposes redemption and resists Carol both actively and passively. Carol is sickened by her own self-righteousness, which she fears will transform her into a priggish, small-minded Gopher Prairie woman; for Lewis, the reform cure is as bad as the sickness of American mediocrity.

Canfield recognized this postwar reaction against activism when she returned from France in 1919, and her impatience with it, in part, motivated *The Brimming Cup. McCall's* capitalized on her new fame and paid her, sight unseen, for a serialized novel. Bessie Beatty, the editor, was a young modern who seemed to amuse both Reynolds and Canfield, who reported that a relative described her as a "nice girl, but only half-baked" (Letter to Reynolds 9 February 1920). Beatty wanted to make her magazine's contents more substantive; Canfield commented after meeting her that "I think her ideas on women's magazines are good, and I respect her trying to do something more than just increase the circulation" (Letter to Reynolds 9 February 1920). Beatty wanted a novel that dealt with the turmoil of the day, including that over the role of marriage. In her advertising for the serialization, she emphasized that the novel was a critique of marriage's validity.

As often happens, Beatty's editorial expectations didn't mesh with Canfield's intentions. Beatty was concerned that the writer would caricature modern radicalism through the character of Eugenia Mills. Canfield responded, "I don't want to use her to make fun of radicalism, which I respect deeply when it is a sincere and honest attempt to improve the conditions of human life, but to make fun of the people who take up radicalism as they did ping-pong, or dancing, because it's the fashion" (Letter to Reynolds 6 February 1920). Interested in getting past the "fashion" of much of the modern revolt, she intended the book as a study of what this new philosophy might actually mean for women.

Beatty's interest in issues and ideas allowed for more than just marriage debates, however; it opened up a space for discussion of race. After the war, race was on Canfield's mind. In 1919, she wrote a story called "An American Citizen," which featured an African American man, brutalized by prejudice in the United States, who creates an exemplary life for himself in France. Despite her fame, she had no success placing this anywhere. She finally sold it for a nominal price to W. E. B. Du Bois for publication in the *Crisis*, and donated the money to a Southern college (Letter to Reynolds 17 February 1920). In *The Brimming Cup*, she returned to this theme, making resistance to race prejudice her model of public activism. Mr. Welles, a retired businessman, goes South to treat African Americans with respect because "the people . . . they're made to suffer all the time for being born the way they are. And that's not right . . . in America" (174). Canfield's relationship with *McCall's* allowed her to bring these sentiments to an audience of millions.

Serialization of *The Brimming Cup* in *McCall's* was just the beginning of the novel's success. *Main Street* and *The Brimming Cup* were, respectively, the number one and number two best-selling novels of the year 1921. Exact figures are difficult to obtain, but the book went through at least four printings, of perhaps twenty thousand copies each, and in 1922, Harcourt, Brace produced a cheap edition of fifty thousand. Canfield wrote to Harcourt, "My—oh! You have certainly known how to sell that book" (Letter to Harcourt 26 October 1922). *Main Street* and *The Brimming Cup* were both widely read and hotly debated.

To critics, the two novels functioned as symbolic antagonists. But Canfield didn't read *Main Street* until after she had completed *The Brimming Cup,* and had not written her novel in direct refutation. She did disagree, though, with much of Lewis's thesis. While praising him for writing a "mighty good novel," she told Alfred Harcourt that "Mr. Lewis takes a rather superficial view of human problems. . . . It is fine to see that a book seriously, honestly, written in an attempt at accuracy and understanding of American life, gets attention and success although there is not a meretricious note in it, nor an insincere one. I don't believe the American public is such a blatant idiot as it is made out" (Letter to Harcourt 10 November 1920). Lewis, for his part, dismissed *The Brimming Cup.* When introduced to Canfield by Harcourt, Lewis reportedly told her, "You are the worst kind of liar" (Yates 90). Canfield, by contrast, praised Lewis for his later work, when he mitigated his disdainful stance toward his subjects—a stance that violated her most deeply held beliefs about authorship. She read *Babbitt* "with the greatest approval" and praised the "real honest pathos and tragedy" of the novel (Letter to Harcourt 9 October 1922).

Reviewers, however, saw the two novels as the epitome of the current cultural debate. In the *Nation,* Freda Kirchway criticized Canfield for providing facile solutions to problems of marriage and traditional values. "If Dorothy Canfield would face the intensity of love and the lure of freedom," she concluded, "as willingly as she faces the reality and depth of family life, she could make a memorable contribution to current thought" (113). Kirchway concluded that Canfield's selective storytelling supported only one side, rigging the outcome of the novel. For Kirchway, "the intensity of love and the lure of freedom" was the more important cultural focus.

In *Collier's Weekly* in 1921, William Allen White termed *The Brimming Cup* "the other side of Main Street." White felt that Canfield had gone beyond surface facts to find the larger truth of the possibilities of village life. "The American country town," he contended, "stands in each book only as a symbol in two contending philosophies" (17). All Americans should first read *Main Street,* White proposed, "to take the conceit out of them" (18), and "then 'The Brimming Cup' should be read as an antidote" (18). For ultimately, White argues,

> Dorothy Canfield's "The Brimming Cup" is a truer book because it takes account of these righteous currents that are moving—however muddily, however sluggishly—moving with the current of progress which is surely directing humanity from a barbarous past to a kindlier, broader, better way of living. (18)

White's analysis, unlike Kirchway's dismissal, embraces both trends in American life as true, but reverses the emphasis. His insistence on the "current of progress" links his criticism and Canfield's novel to Progressive politics before the Great War. Unlike Lewis, who dismisses activism, Canfield has found a way to bring it into the world of women's magazines.

Formally, *The Brimming Cup* is a hybrid. It employs a simplified Jamesian style of interior monologue. Canfield provides characters, like Marise, with whom readers can identify, and plot devices to hold their interest, including love triangles, murderous jealousy, and possible adultery; her interest in psychological drama does not preclude willingness to give her readers a good story. One critic observed, "Mrs. Fisher . . . employs vivid events and emotional scenes. But when she resorts to these expedients, she uses them in established ways. She gains her effects in old ways brought down to date, not in new ways" (Boynton 298). In her adaptation of popular forms, Canfield worked hard to make her writing seem transparent.

In *The Brimming Cup,* Canfield turns a small Vermont town into complicated and transformed American cultural terrain. To represent the diversity of perspectives within the larger culture, she uses third-person narrative but employs the limited viewpoints of a variety of characters, including the eight-year-old Elly. This multiple narration is a common feature in Canfield's writing; she especially likes to focus on those whom others consider inarticulate, even moronic, to show how little we understand those around us. (For example, in her 1933 *Bonfire,* a cat, Henrietta, articulates the novel's primary theme of sex and civilization.) The reader must draw conclusions and make judgments based on these limited perspectives, as in real life; Canfield as novelist provides insight into each character's true motivations. Rarely are characters' perceptions of each other accurate. Vincent Marsh, the New York modern, considers eight-year-old Elly a brooding, clinging animal, and Nelly (a local femme fatale) a symbol of inarticulate sensuality; but other passages show Elly's insight and Nelly's sexless practicality. One character sums up the novel's fictional logic: "I don't know that *any*thing is the truth. I should say that both of you told the truth about it. The truth's pretty big for any one person to tell" (84). Perspective determines truth, and the more one is committed to a particular worldview, the less one is likely to see.

Different vocabularies, Canfield argues, produce different realities; children at a dance with their parents, as Marise, the heroine, conjectures, may show that "households are in such a low and lamentably primitive condition that they haven't any slave-labour to leave the children with, and so bring them along out of mere brute necessity" but, "in another vocabulary," she explains, their presence shows "a close feeling of family unity, and [that] they *like* to have their children with them when they are having a good time, and find it pleasant to see mothers dancing with their little boys and fathers with their little girls" (117). Both perspectives are valid; neither can entirely account for the "truth." And yet, the larger truth of Canfield's writing is the innate goodness and potential of human beings. If we can learn to read people with as much concentration and care as we read texts, she suggests, we will be become better citizens, parents, and friends.

The plot of *The Brimming Cup* provides intrigue and melodrama to hold the reader's attention and engage her politically and socially. The novel begins with Marise and Neale as passionate young lovers who have met in Italy, then jumps eleven years to Marise's prosaic life as a housewife with three children in a small Vermont town. The appearance of the New York millionaire Vincent Marsh coincides with her awakening to discontentment. The main drama centers around Marise's attraction to Vincent and her temptation to leave the stolid Neale for a life of glamour, passion, and ease.

Other supporting characters include Eugenia Mills, Marise's childhood friend who is wealthy, self-indulgent, and trivial, and whose obsession for Neale creates an love triangle overlapping that of Marise, Neale, and Vincent; Nelly and Gene Powers, a mismatched couple in yet another (perceived) love triangle that acts as a foil to that of Marise, Neale, and Vincent; Aunt Hetty, whose death precipitates Marise's final decision; Marise's three children, constant symbols of her discontent and her purpose; and Mr. Welles, a retired businessman who sees his retreat to Vermont as a defeat and who gradually discovers new strength. Interlocking subplots help Canfield to transform a stock romantic device into more encompassing human drama.

She further extends the significance of her story beyond individual tragedy to the universal human condition by embedding big cultural questions as key factors in Marise's choice between two lovers: a Freudian emphasis on desire and the pathology of motherhood; the role of labor and the increasing stratification of classes; the continuing problem of race in America; the definition of culture and its meaning and importance in a democracy. Canfield thus transforms the story of a marriage saved into a progressive promise of a nation healed and redeemed.

Marise's discontent is personal, for the intense passion she once shared with her husband has faded into easy familiarity. But the significance of that commonplace phenomenon is heightened by postwar disillusionment. Vincent expresses this feeling: World War I demonstrates the bankruptcy of political optimism, self-sacrifice, and public service. The only truth for Vincent is death; pleasure is his only diversion. Canfield reveals his utter despair, his nihilism, in an interior monologue representative of the "lost" generation:

> The blackness dropped deeper about him, and within him. There they were dancing, those idiots, dancing on a volcano if ever human being did, in the little sultry respite from the tornado which was called the world-peace. Well, that was less idiotic than working, at least. How soon before it would break again, the final destructive hurricane, born of nothing but the malignant folly of human hearts, and sweep away all that they now agonized and sweated to keep?

> What silly weakness to spend the respite in anything but getting as much of what you wanted as you could, before it was all gone in the big final smash-up, and the yellow or black man were on top. (120)

Uncertainty, nativism, imminent apocalypse—these are the legacies of post–World War I disillusionment in *The Brimming Cup.* Underneath the sensual abandon, Canfield implies, is an infectious despair—and malignant racism.

Vincent rejects activism for pleasure, a refuge that he believes only money can provide. Desire is his raison d'etre; he proclaims, "It is the only honestly living thing in all our miserable human life, the passion of a man and a woman for each other. It is the only thing that moves us out of our cowardly lethargy of dead-and-alive egotism" (226). Freudian insistence on the primacy of passion, Canfield suggests, came into vogue after the war because it seemed the only means to a transcendent, communal experience.

Marise fears that such thoughts "shake the very foundation of our life" (185). She doubts her marriage and her motherhood because she doubts the possibility of activism and change. Vincent, again spokesman for the moderns, leads this assault on the value of activism:

> It's Harold-bellwrightism, pure and simple, to imagine that anything you can ever do, that anybody can ever do, will help bring about the kind of order *you're* talking about, order for everybody. The only kind of order there will ever be, is what you get when you grab a little of what you want out of the chaos, for your own self, while there's still time, and hold on to it. That's the only way to get anywhere for yourself. And as for doing something for other people, the only satisfaction you can give anybody is in beauty. (73)

In a world of chaos, self-gratification is the only constant; "beauty" the only civic action. Marise confesses that she longs for the moments when she "feel[s] as though my life were part of something much bigger than just *my* life" (146). The denouement of World War I makes her doubt this impulse. Its "holy principles" and "sacred cause" have devolved into imperialist payback. Echoing Vincent, she wonders, "Could it have been worse if we had all just grabbed what we could get for ourselves, and had what satisfaction we could out of baser pleasures?" (100). She wonders whether activism itself is to blame: "What could one feel except Melancholy at the sight of the world of humanity, poor world, war-ridden, broken in health, ruined in hope, the very nerves of action cut by the betrayal of its desperate efforts to be something more than base?" (102). For Marise, disillusioned by the war and discontented with her life, Vincent's cynicism contains enough truth for her to question her own commitment, however small, to familial and social responsibilities. If, as he claims, "the only honestly living thing in all our miserable human life" is "the passion of a man and a woman for each other" (226), all else is negligible. Marise's crisis of faith, then, concerns the very possibility of social change. Her personal commitments, and larger American commitments to equality and justice, are inextricably linked.

Through a conventional seduction tale, Canfield thus connects sexuality with larger cultural and social issues. What Marise needs, and what by analogy her readers need, is an alternative basis for faith, one not dependent upon religion or upon hypocritical platitudes, but upon something tangible and sustainable. Passion alone, contrary to Vincent's assertion, does not allow people to transcend themselves. Canfield's solutions in *The Brimming Cup* are art, activism, and republican motherhood.

Deweyan art as experience is here a counter to Vincent and Eugenia's class-bound sense of culture. Marise loves Beethoven and quotes Goethe; this is what first drew Vincent to her. But she identifies Eugenia's culture fetish as deriving from a peculiarly American inferiority complex.

> No European could ever take culture so seriously. You know how any convert always has a thousand times more fervour than the fatigued members of the faith who were born to it. . . . I have always envied Henry James the conviction he seems to have had, all his life, that Europeans are a good deal more unlike other people than I ever found them. It may be obtuseness on my part, but I never could see that people who lived in the Basses-Pyrenees are any more cultivated or had any broader horizons than people who live in the Green Mountains. My own experience is that when you actually live with people day after day, year after year, you find about the same range of possibilities in any group of them. (45)

Marise's attitude debunks the idea that Americans are without, in Van Wyck Brooks's diagnosis, a "usable past," thus without culture or taste.

Marise here echoes Canfield's own perspective (Letter to Harcourt 10 November 1920). Ordinary people may not appreciate Vincent's highbrow tastes, but they do experience aesthetics as Dewey supposes.

One striking aesthetic experience in the novel is the flowering of the cereus, a "crabbed, ungainly plant-creature" that blooms once a year, for one day, "a wonderful exotic flower of extreme beauty" (*Brimming Cup* 80). Everyone in the town, "tired from their day's struggle with the earth," goes to see this phenomenon, which is a metaphor for the role a pragmatist aesthetic can play in the lives of ordinary people:

> One big, shining petal was slowly, slowly, but quite visibly uncurling at the tip. From that moment on, she saw nothing, felt nothing but the opening flower, lived only in the incredibly leisurely, masterful motion with which the grotesquely shaped protecting petals curled themselves back from the centre. Their motion was so slow that the mind was lost in dreaminess in following it. Had that last one moved? No, it stood, still, poised breathlessly . . . and yet, there before them, revealed, exultant, the starry heart of the great flower shimmered in the lamplight. (82)

Marise is as moved by the blooming of the flower as she is by Beethoven or Goethe—perhaps more, because this experience is valued by everyone in the town, not just a favored few. Vincent, of course, dismisses the significance of this "rite of the worship of beauty," terming it a freak show for "dull, insensitive, primitive beings" who "would infinitely prefer a two-headed calf or a bearded woman to your flower" (84). Marise must learn to fight modern questioning and affirm the reality of what she experienced.

Marise discovers a form of aesthetic fulfillment unknown to Vincent and Eugenia when she shares a democratized culture with the laborers of Ashley. Directing the men's chorus, she guides them to embrace the music and feels the joy of communion:

> For a moment there hung before her eyes the powerful, roughly clad bodies of those vigorous men, their weatherbeaten faces, their granite impassivity, under which her eye had caught the triumph of the moment, warming them as it did her, with the purest of joys this side of heaven, the consciousness of having made music worthily. The

> whole valley seemed to be filled to its brim with that shout of exultation. It had taken all of her patience, and will-power, and knowledge of her art and of these people to achieve that moment. But it had lifted her high, high above the smallness of life, up to a rich realm of security and joy. (316)

Canfield appropriates religious language to describe the workmen's secular appreciation of art. In this Deweyan experience is a basis for faith.

Activism is another basis for faith, but one that must be reimagined. Caught in the larger cultural backlash against World War I and the Progressive impulses that justified it, Marise has lost faith in the ability of reform to change anything. She feels "terribly fooled with our idealistic hopes about the war" (103), and wonders whether "we are being fooled again when we try for the higher planes of life." It may be, she concludes, that "those people are right who say that to grab for the pleasure of the senses is the best," for her humanism is badly shaken.

Mr. Welles, by contrast, has been crushed by American industrialism. He has "detested the sort of 'life' he'd experienced in business" (28), because "the only reality in the world of men" is that "if you didn't cut the other fellow's throat first he would cut yours" (132). He is grateful to have escaped this to the "pleasant gentle, slightly unreal world of women, nice women, and children and gardens," but he feels himself a failure for giving up.

Neale helps Mr. Welles by proposing that business is not social Darwinism but a kind of public service. But what finally rouses Mr. Welles is what most people in Ashley, Marise included, dismiss as the "Negro problem." A letter from his niece about the indignities suffered by African Americans in the South enrages him, and he takes countering them as a personal and American responsibility. In his inarticulate way, he explains his reasoning to Marise's son Paul:

> The coloured people . . . they're made to suffer all the time for being born the way they are. And that's not right . . . in America. . . . Americans that happen to be coloured people ought to have every bit of the same chance to amount to their best that any Americans have. . . . That wrong feeling about coloured people, not wanting them to be respected as much as any American, is . . . that's a tree that's got to come down. I'm too old to take an axe to it. And, any-

> how, if you cut that sort of thing down with an axe, the roots generally live and start all over again. If we can just wash the ground out from under it, with enough people thinking differently, maybe it'll fall, roots and all, of its own weight. (175–177)

Mr. Welles, at the end of his life and after all his disappointments, finds a belief that can sustain him. His model of social change—ordinary people washing the ground out from under the tree of racism—embraces progress and Progressive politics.

Initially, Marise is outraged by what seems to her Mr. Welles's masochistic pleasure in sacrifice: "He's going to do harm, in all probability, mix up a situation already complicated beyond solution, and why is he? So that he can indulge himself in the perverse pleasure of the rasp of a hair-shirt" (224). And Vincent draws an analogy between Mr. Welles's self-sacrifice and Marise's resistance to having an affair, finding both pointless.

Two contrasting letters at the end of the novel, however, demonstrate activism's sustaining power. Eugenia, with the whole world at her disposal, is consumed by ennui, and moans that "There is no corner of the modern world which is not vulgar and common. Democracy has done its horrible leveling down with a vengeance" (317–318). Mr. Welles, by contrast, finds fulfillment in his embrace of humanism and reform:

> I'm just swept back into youth again. It makes me very much mortified when I think what a corking good time I am having and what sanctimonious martyr's airs I put on about coming down here. . . . Working as I am, nobody feels about me the laid-on-the shelf compassion which everybody (and me too) was feeling before. I *am* somebody here. (318)

Experiential art and activism become fused, for Marise, in the role of motherhood. Sentimental culture was transfixed by the sublimity of motherhood, and as Ann Douglas argues, the Victorian matriarch both appalled and transfixed the moderns, who desperately attacked her to break her spell. Vincent consistently assails motherhood as a dangerous, unnecessary, outmoded concept. He compares it to drug addiction; they are "two different ways of getting away from reality" (99). Marriage, "a ghastly prison" (18), and motherhood are "the Chinese shoes of outworn ideas" (86) which prevent Marise from the complete fulfillment of passion. Vincent attacks her naiveté:

> You can't pretend to be sincere in trying to pull that antimacassar home and mother stuff on me. Ask Bernard, Shaw, ask Freud, ask Mrs. Gilman, how good it is for children's stronger, better selves to live in the enervating, host-house concentration on them of an unbalanced, undeveloped woman, who has let everything else in her personality atrophy except her morbid preoccupation with her own offspring. That's really the meaning of what's sentimentally called "mothering." (86)

It is this attack on the value of motherhood that ultimately drives Marise into crisis, for all this questioning "shakes the very foundations of our life" (185). And there is enough truth in Vincent's accusation to keep her wondering.

This critique of motherhood is not just about sexuality, however; it is also about class. Housewives, especially housewives in small towns, exist as a sort of amalgam of upper and lower classes; their husbands' prosperity frees them from outside work, yet they labor at recurrent, often thankless tasks. When, early in the novel, Marise dismisses Vincent's reference to the "big world" and asserts that "your world everywhere is about as big as you are," Vincent emphasizes class and privilege:

> Mr. Marsh eyed her hard, and shook his head, with a little scornful downward thrust of the corners of his mouth, as though he were an augur who refused to lend himself to the traditional necessity to keep up the appearance of believing in an exploded religion. "*You* know where the big world is," he said firmly. "It's where there are only people who don't have to work, who have plenty of money and brains and beautiful possessions and gracious ways of living, and few moral scruples. (47–48)

Real life, by this definition, exists only for the few who don't have to work; the majority are left out. In rejecting motherhood, Vincent rejects "moral scruples" and menial, trivial details, to him the antithesis of "culture." Marise, it seems, must choose between them to find fulfillment and freedom.

Canfield extricates her from this quandary by revising the terms of the debate. The moderns' sexual liberation imprisons women; motherhood heals industrialism's breach between labor and intellect, poor and rich. In the midst of heated debates about the New Woman, Canfield offers a compelling argument about the position of women in the "modern" consciousness. New women are really not new at all; as usual, women are valued only for their ability to inflame and gratify male desire. Modern ideas about the primacy of passion enslave them as much as the nineteenth-century cult of true womanhood did.

Neale, whomVincent thinks an unimaginative and boorish husband, understands that women are more than their ability to arouse desire, and respects Marise's integrity and autonomy in a way that the passionate lover Vincent—who desires mastery—never does. He perceives the problem of this modern overemphasis on passion:

> That notion, solemnly accepted by the would-be sophisticated moderns, for instance, that a woman of beauty and intelligence was being wasted unless she was engaged in being the "emotional inspiration" of some man's life: which meant in plain English, stimulating his sexual desire to that fever-heat which they called impassioned living. As if there were not a thousand other forms of deep fulfillment in life. (158)

In fact, Canfield shows that Vincent's desire for Marise is really a desire for possession. An indication of Marise's discontent and pliability causes him to respond in triumph: "The deep, fundamental, inalienable need for possession stretched itself, titanic and mighty" (157). He wants her to yield, to tremble, to be plucked. Marise must choose not between duty and passion but between autonomy and submission.

It is a new concept of communal motherhood that offers Marise the greatest autonomy and fulfillment. This modernized republican motherhood insists that men should become more like women—communal, nurturing, and responsible—rather than women "modernizing" themselves to become more like men selfish, promiscuous, and irresponsible. Housewives, in fact, have a keen connection to the "reality" the moderns so desperately seek, because they work with their hands. Marriage and motherhood can bridge the gap between upper and lower classes, a gap most clearly defined as between leisure and labor. Marise has been attracted to Vincent because he promises to save her from labor:

> There had been many parts to this: her revolt from the mere physical drudgery of her life, from giving so much of her strength to the dull, unsavoury, material things. This summer, a thousand times in a thousand ways, there had been brought home to her by Vincent, by Eugenia, the fact that there were lives so arranged that other people did all the drudgery, and left one free to perceive nothing but the beauty and delicacy of existence. (265)

Marise concludes, though, that "freedom from drudgery" does not "give them a keener sense of the beauty and delicacy of existence." Rather, separation from common humanity makes them less satisfied, more addicted to despair as a stimulant that obscures the ennui of their lives.

It seems to Marise that all should share in manual labor, for it is ennobling and real:

> The existence in the world of so much drudgery and unlovely slavery to material processes was an insoluble mystery; but a life in which her part of it would be taken by other people and added to their own burdens . . . no, she had grown into something which could not endure that!
>
> Perhaps this was one of the hard, unwelcome lessons that the war had brought to her. . . . The bitterness of those days had shocked her imagination alive to the shame of sharing and enjoying what she had not helped to pay for, to the disharmony of having more than your share while other people have less than theirs. (266–267)

In this egalitarian vision, people do their own work and share both burdens and pleasures equally. Marise's life as a mother, seemingly self-interested and narrow, is her way of "taking her share."

The Brimming Cup, then, modernizes republican motherhood. Self-sacrifice and impersonal commitment are best for Marise, but not because women are by nature more spiritual and selfless than men. Rather, her development from personal gratification to larger self-sacrifice represents growth into maturity, the claiming of adult responsibilities and adult autonomy. But even more, motherhood transforms her private responsibilities into a public trust, providing the model for involved citizenship. Through motherhood, Marise transcends her own limitations:

> Her heart swelled and opened wide to a conception of something greater and deeper in motherhood than she had had; but which she could have if she could deserve it; something so wide and sun-flooded that the old selfish, possessive, never-satisfied ache which had called itself love withered away, its power to hurt and poison her gone. (269)

She finds herself able to embrace Mr. Welles's quixotic journey South, and cares for Ralph Powers, whose parents have tragically died, because "any child who needed a mother so much was *her own child*" (307). Now Marise "had at last stepped outside the narrow circle of personal desire, and found all the world open to her" (289). Motherhood promotes not apolitical personalism, but a political personalism, if you will.

In true Deweyan fashion, Marise must look to herself and her own experience as the only valid authority, and she realizes that life with Neale will allow her to be who she is most completely. All outside advice must be ignored, especially that of the clamorous new Greenwich Village crowd, whose radical prescriptions seem most designed to keep her from hearing her own voice.

> Push back all those thick-clustering, intruding, distracting traditional ideas of other people on both sides; the revolt on one hand, the feeble resignation on the other; what other women did; what people had said. . . . This was *her* life, *her* question, hers alone. . . . But at this there came a wild protesting clamour, bursting out to prevent her from completing this thought; loud, urgent voices, men's, women's. . . . They cried her down as a traitor to the fullness of life. . . . Only disconnected words reached her, but she recognized the well-known sentences from which they came . . . "puritanism . . . abundance of personality . . . freedom of development . . . nothing else vital in human existence . . . prudishness . . . Conventionality . . . our only possibly contact with the life-purpose . . . with the end of passion life declines and dies." (276–277)

The trendy catchphrases are simply another set of prescriptions that can prevent women from choosing their own lives; but none of them necessarily have anything to do with her. Nor should conventional considerations—including the effect of a divorce on her children—prevail; all that matters, as Neale tells her, is "what is best for you." The truth resides only within Marise, and it leads her out of herself. Canfield thus recuperates American individualism to connect the middle-class mother's interconnectedness to the larger ideals of American democracy.

Popular Feminism and Progressive Middlebrow

Canfield's politics incorporate the contradictions of the larger Progressive movement.[5] Yet even in confirming her readers' most treasured prejudices, she insists on a Progressive vision of America—with equality and individualism at the center. Her Dewey-influenced writing seeks to create a democratic national culture undivided by class, race, and sex. In the end, she treats her predominantly female readership like the thinking, independent citizens she believes they can become.

This embrace of middle-class readers and faith in their essential goodness contrasts with the better-known critical mode of "terrible honesty," which denounced the cancer it found beneath the hypocritical platitudes of the class. H. L. Mencken caricatured that enemy as an insidious "mushy multitude,"

> that huge body of honest and right-thinking folk which constitute the heart, lungs and bowels of this great republic—that sturdy multitude which believes in newspapers, equinoctial storms, trust-busting, the Declaration of Independence, teleology, the direct primary, the uplift, trial by jury, monogamy, the Weather Bureau, Congress and the moral order of the world—that innumerable caravan of middling, dollar-grubbing, lodge-joining, quack-ridden folk which the Socialists sneer at loftily as the *bourgeoisie,* the politicians slobber over as the bulwark of our liberties. (Nolte 167)

Mencken's attack on the "mushy multitude" rejects democracy as a sort of opiate of the masses. Certainly what "the folk" have been capable of throughout American history, including lynching and racial discrimination, might seem to justify his scorn and dismissal.

But what Canfield holds out is a faith in the ability to experiment and to improve what already exists—a legacy of the Progressive movement and Deweyan political and aesthetic theories. Her articulation of progressive middlebrow aesthetics provided a model for women's activist writing throughout the interwar period.

TWO

Miscegenating Middlebrow

Jessie Fauset and the "Authentic" Black Middle Class

In 1933, after reading Alain Locke's review of her fourth and last novel, *Comedy: American Style,* Jessie Fauset fired off a scathing letter, capping at least a decade of resentment and competitive hostility, which said in part:

> I have always disliked your attitude toward my work dating from the time years ago when you went out of your way to tell my brother that the dinner given at the Civic Club for "There Is Confusion" wasn't for me. Incidentally I may tell you now that the idea originated with Regina Anderson and Gwendolyn Bennett, both members of a little literary club with which I was then associated. How you and one or two others sought to distort the idea and veil its original graciousness. . . . And I still remember the consummate cleverness with which you that night as toastmaster strove to keep speech and comment away from the person for whom the occasion was meant. . . .
>
> But today's article is positively the worst because in it you have shown yourself so clearly as a subscriber to that purely Negroid school whose motto is "whatever is white is right." . . .
>
> But in the case of Mr. McKay and myself—our few virtues are barely outlined, our faults greatly stressed and in my own case I

> am left with[out] a leg to stand on. Characterization, style, sentiment, treatment are all wrong. My art is "slowly maturing"; my "championship of upper and middle class Negro life" is not even "singlehanded"; it is "*almost* singlehanded." And what does such an expression as this mean—"Her characterization is too close to type?"—Just nothing! I was telling the story of a real family—how could it be a story of types?
>
> One last point—The one that made me most furious—I wasn't telling the story of "one dark child in a family" etc. If I had been even I, poor mid-Victorian, sentimental persevering Miss Fauset, would have told the story from a different angle. I was telling the story of a woman who was obsessed with the desire for whiteness.
>
> And would you kindly, Alain, send me pages on which Mid-Victorian style prevails. . . .
>
> No dear Alain, your malice, your lack of true discrimination and above all your tendency to play safe with the grand white folks renders you anything but a reliable critic. Better stick to your own field and let us writers alone. At least I can tell a story convincingly. (Letter to Locke 9 January 1933)

One can trace here the competing claims and hopes of the Harlem Renaissance: social transformation and individual freedom; folk art and literature; experimentation and accessibility; authenticity and assimilation. What is most striking, however, is how Fauset reverses common critical assumptions about "authentic" black writing. It is Alain Locke—editor of *The New Negro,* master of ceremonies at the semiofficial launch of the Harlem Renaissance—who has pandered to white expectations, and Jessie Fauset—literary editor of the *Crisis,* middle-class spinster, and author of four "mid-Victorian" women's novels—who has rejected the "grand white folks" to represent an authentic picture of African American life.

Locke's version of the Harlem Renaissance has endured, while Fauset is remembered mainly as a footnote. Even critics who reclaim her must address the "problem" of her middle-class identity and her novels that seem painfully old-fashioned next to vernacular triumphs by Langston Hughes and Zora Neale Hurston. This is true not only of African American male critics, but of many feminist critics as well.[1]

Fauset's letter suggests that her writing was not a failure of New Negro philosophy but the product of conscious choices. It points to another Harlem Renaissance, one less concerned with formal innovation and cultural rebellion than with the needs and pleasures of "race" men and women. Jessie Fauset's Harlem Renaissance challenges cultural, aesthetic, and racial assumptions on which much of our contemporary critical tradition depends. In this chapter, I will examine Fauset's career in terms of her Progressive activism. Rather than reclaim Fauset in spite of her fiction, as Cheryl Wall does (36), I want to connect her investment in activism and literary societies with the mode of authorship she embraced.

"There's No Future for a Black Writer": Construction of Authorship

Jessie Fauset, born three years after Dorothy Canfield, shares many of her aesthetic and political commitments. Like Canfield, Fauset could trace her family's American roots back to the 1700s through her family Bible (Sylvander 25). Both were thoroughly immersed in the politics of the Progressive era, including racial equality, education, and the liberalism of John Dewey (though Fauset's exposure came indirectly through W. E. B. Du Bois). Fauset's father was an African Methodist Episcopal minister who held a prominent position as a "cultural leader" in black Philadelphia (24). Education and uplift were emphasized in her home (26, 27), and she sought out the best education possible in Philadelphia, which meant attending predominantly white schools. Despite serious racial prejudice, she was one of very few African Americans to attend the prestigious Philadelphia High School for Girls. According to her brother, "Long years after graduation, like Alain Locke at Pedagogy, her name was a by-word for scholastic brilliance. At her graduation the school had honored her by inviting her father to give the invocation—an unusual token of esteem" (Huff Fauset 72). Graduating valedictorian, however, wasn't enough to win her acceptance to Bryn Mawr, whose president, M. Carey Thomas, worried more about offending white Southerners than about honoring Fauset's academic record. Only the intervention of *Philadelphia Press* editor Talcott Williams led to her acceptance at Cornell University. Fauset was one of a handful of black women to receive a B.A. degree in 1905 from Cornell, where she graduated Phi Beta Kappa in 1905, the first African American woman to do so. A later Master's degree from the University of Pennsylvania made her one of the most educated black women of her day.

Fauset continued to emphasize education. She was a teacher at Paul Laurence Dunbar High School in Washington, D.C., a school with a remarkably talented faculty: two other members were among the first black women to receive doctorates, in 1921 (Wall 43). She edited a children's magazine for African Americans in the twenties. Even her role as "midwife" to the Harlem Renaissance shows this passion for education; her correspondence with the poets who would become major figures of the new movement reads like tutelage.

Education, however, was a double-edged sword. College had confirmed her faith in education's value (Huff Fauset 71), yet her education did not provide her with the opportunity it did her white classmates. Fauset was barred from most professions, except teaching. Despite extraordinary connections in New York and an impressive career as the literary editor of the *Crisis,* she was unable to find employment anywhere in New York in 1927, and had to return to the classroom in her late forties. Even her teaching options were severely limited; she wasn't allowed to teach in the segregated school system in Philadelphia, which is why she moved to Washington (71)—and why Dunbar High School had such an impressive black faculty. In Washington, Fauset moved in diplomatic circles, primarily Latin American and French, and knew African American scholars like Sterling Brown (74). She lived on the borders of power, within a self-sufficient African American community.

The limits of education prompted Fauset's engagement with Progressive causes in the first decades of the century. Through the NAACP she investigated discrimination cases in higher education. Her interest in racial equality became, her biographer suggests, enmeshed with other social movements of the Progressive era (Sylvander 39). She was heavily involved in the production of the *Crisis,* for which she served as literary editor part-time in 1911; after moving to New York in 1919, she managed the weekly in the editor's absence.

The editor, of course, was W. E. B. Du Bois, who had a profound influence on Fauset both professionally and personally. Du Bois had studied pragmatism with William James at Harvard; George Hutchinson argues that James's focus on results and the "cash-value" of ideas led to Du Bois's shift from philosophy to social science and, eventually, to the social activism of the NAACP (36). As the chief opponent of Booker T. Washington's segregated, industrial vision of "Negroes," Du Bois loomed large as a public figure in the Progressive era after the publication of *The Souls of Black Folk* in 1903. A brilliant sociology scholar at Atlanta University, one of the few black institutions that taught anything but industrial education, Du Bois used the success of *The Souls of Black Folk* to establish a counterbalance to Washington, publishing articles in magazines like the *Century* and *Collier's*. His later work for the NAACP, which was founded in 1910, put him in the national spotlight.

Du Bois emphasized culture as one of many important political fronts. He insisted, influenced by pragmatist aesthetics, that fiction could transform hearts and minds and create vicarious experiences that could be used for political ends. Later, his position hardened, against what he saw as Harlem Renaissance decadence, into the dogmatism that "all art is propaganda, and ever must be, despite the wailing of the purists" (quoted in Lewis *W. E. B. Du Bois: The Fight for Equality* 175). Fauset, despite her more literary predilections, saw art as promoting racial equality, even as she rejected the charge that it was all propaganda

Jessie Fauset was inspired by *The Souls of Black Folk*, and she wrote Du Bois a gushing letter of appreciation. He would become an important mentor. He encouraged her fiction writing, read drafts of her novels, wrote influential reviews, and even arranged for reprintings of her novels. It is easy to overemphasize Fauset's relationship to Du Bois,[2] as David Levering Lewis does. Fauset was more than simply a Du Bois lackey and mistress. Ongoing communities of women readers and writers were equally important in her work.

Fauset was exposed both to the "great books" of the genteel tradition and to the more political writings of abolitionists and black activists. Harriet Beecher Stowe was one of her earliest encounters, which she described years later to the readers of the *Crisis:*

> What I did read with interest, with amazement, with resentment, with tears, was "Uncle Tom's Cabin." It lay a grayish brown volume, thick-leaved and large lettered on the kidney-shaped table in our parlor. It belonged to my grandmother whom I had never seen. . . . But on a certain Christmas Day, weary of Rose-Red and Snow-White, I happened to peep within those prim covers. They had to pry the book from my unwilling fingers. At the end of three or four days I had read it all, every word of it. I do not think I have ever opened it since but the story remains part of my permanent mental furnishings. ("When Christmas Comes" 62)

Fauset's encounter with *Uncle Tom's Cabin* epitomizes the middlebrow reading experience. Despite a lifetime of disappointments, one still had to pry books from Fauset's unwilling fingers; even at the end she had not given up hope that she would become a successful writer.

That first passionate experience established a long apprenticeship for Fauset as a reader. She savored the ornate prose of the Victorians. In a letter to Du Bois in 1907, she cataloged her favorite writers:

> Off in one of the little side-rooms stands my desk, covered with books that have caught my special fancy and awakened my thoughts. This is my *living*-room, where I pass my moods of bitterness and misunderstanding, and questioning and joy, too, I think. Often in the midst of a heap of books—the Rubaiyat and a Bible, Walter Pater's Essays, and "Robert Elsmere" and "Aurora Leigh," and books of belief, of insinuation, of open unbelief, —I bow my head on my desk in a passion of doubt and ignorance and longing, and ponder, ponder. Here on this desk is a book in which I jot down all the little, beautiful word-wonders whose truest meanings are so often unknown to me, but whose very mystery I love. . . . High up on many of the shelves in the many rooms are books as yet unread by me, Schopenhauer and Tolstoi, Petrarch and Sappho, Goethe and Kant and Schilling. . . . With such reading in store for me, is not my future rich? (Letter to Du Bois 27 February 1907)

Fauset's catalog of her rich future is an early version of the "Great Books" of the nineteenth century; Walter Pater, Schopenhauer, Tolstoy, Petrarch, Sappho, Goethe, Kant, Schilling, Elizabeth Barrett Browning, and Mrs. Humphry (Mary Augusta) Ward. Pater is particularly important, for he was known for beautiful, florid prose. Fauset claimed him as her most enduring model, because "I have always liked words—and appreciate and differentiate their grouping" (Letter to Jean Toomer 24 February 1922).

Fauset's pleasure in reading was passionate, sensual, and deeply engaged; her love of the "mystery" of "all the little, beautiful word-wonders" speaks of an aesthetic embracing form and content equally. Like Dewey and Canfield, she fetishized the book and worshipped at the shrine of culture; but she also made of that "culture" a tool of liberation. Most telling about this cataloguing of books is that it is not only primarily European but highbrow. That Fauset could identify with cultures and experiences so removed from her own likely persuaded her that literature had the power to bridge the seemingly insurmountable. It might even have some effect on race prejudice in America.

This faith in literature's power, in fact, was central to much of the larger agenda of Progressive African Americans. Women's reading groups, as Elizabeth McHenry details in *Forgotten Readers,* made self-education in the classics central to their political and cultural ambitions. For these women, "literature resurfaced as one of the practical tools black Americans envisioned using not only to reflect but also in fact to redefine themselves and their roles in the larger community" (188). "Interaction with print," McHenry continues, was a potential vehicle for constructing identity and regulating social change that carried with it the power to elevate and enlighten the race" (188). Women in literary clubs were to become, Victoria Earle Matthews charged in 1895, "literary activists" who embraced and created "race literature" that corrected the malignant stereotypes of white America" (quoted in McHenry 190, 191). By creating and reading literature, black women would "reap the benefits of its stature" (191).

Jessie Fauset's participation in such literary societies in the first decade of the twentieth century is likely. Her reading strategies match theirs and her connections at Dunbar High School would have given her access to some of the best minds in African American culture. Her later involvement in Georgia Douglas Johnson's literary society the Saturday Nighters in the 1920s (McHenry 274) and in New York with younger poets and playwrights like Regina Andrews and Gwendolyn Bennett also suggests a commitment to literary societies.

Langston Hughes and Arthur Huff Fauset, Jessie's brother, described these salons at her house. Fauset's "literary teas," Huff Fauset wrote, were "jolly affairs, where members of the black middle class, chiefly paid homage to the black writer whom they esteemed not only for her literary competence, but as a friend and social companion; many of these were wives of physicians, lawyers, business men (like her husband) and studies whose parents were of the black bourgeoisie" (quoted in Sylvander 78). The readership she imagined for her articles, poems, and novels was based on these intimate gatherings of educated African Americans, who, Hughes tells us, read poetry, talked literature, and spoke in French (quoted in Sylvander 78). These quasi-private affairs represent a model for the relationship between reader and writer endemic to middlebrow authorship.

Fauset possessed models not just of readers but of African American authors in her adolescence and early twenties. Her novels were unmistakably influenced by predecessors like Frances Ellen Watkins Harper's *Iola Leroy* (1892)and Pauline Hopkins's *Contending Forces* (1900). The Philadelphia novelist Frances Harper published in AME journals, and it is unthinkable that Fauset, the daughter of an AME minister in Philadelphia, was not exposed to her formidable influence. Pauline Hopkins also had the ear of educated African Americans, through her editorship of the *Colored American.* Fauset secularized the Social Gospel aims of these writers, but she kept their narrative interest in romance and in racial "passing" and their earnest desire for social transformation through their writing.

Harper and Hopkins wrote primarily for black audiences, supplemented by liberal whites. But during Fauset's apprenticeship years, she encountered writers who were able to reach white audiences as well. Charles W. Chestnutt appropriated the local- color tradition to write for the *Atlantic Monthly;* William Dean Howells promoted the stories that later formed Chesnutt's *The Conjure Woman (1899).* Paul Laurence Dunbar also had a strong literary reputation at the turn of the century, reading for presidents, publishing poetry and articles in white mainstream publications, and receiving considerable remuneration for his published works. Both were ultimately limited by the white public's preference for dialect and colorful Negro characters. Yet both provided models of black writers who were able to command part of the considerable profits of Progressive publishing and influence a broader American audience.

Despite this intense immersion in reading and writing, however, Fauset didn't publish her first novel until 1924, when she was forty-two, a mystery of sorts to scholars. Du Bois certainly found it so, and was exasperated with what he perceived as her recalcitrance. Arthur Huff Fauset offers his own explanation on his half-sister'sdelay. On visits to her "passing" siblings in Philadelphia, he wrote,

> Often, however, she mentioned how she pined to be writing stories and novels and poems, instead of standing before reluctant classes of black boys and girls, trying to pump into their brains the intricacies of Latin syntax or endeavoring to get them to produce the awkward

> sounding French vowels. She would sigh and exclaim, "But there's no future for a black writer! (Huff Fauset 91)

"No future for a black writer": the claim, at first, seems outrageous, given the plethora of writings by and about African Americans in the Progressive boom. In an era that produced Chesnutt, Hopkins, Harper, and most importantly Du Bois, what could Fauset have meant?

We may have the beginnings of an answer in the autobiography of one of Fauset's friends from Washington, Mary Church Terrell. A dedicated race woman, the first African American on the Washington, D.C. school board, Terrell spends a chapter in *A Colored Woman in a White World* mourning her thwarted literary ambitions. Although McHenry ascribes her failure to too many political and family commitments, Terrell points to prejudice against activism and against politically inflected writing. "All of my stories," she tells us, "were based on the Race Problem," and she "soon discovered that there are few things more difficult than inducing an editor of the average magazine to publish an article on the Race Problem, unless it sets forth the point of view which is popularly and generally accepted" (224). She elaborates:

> Nobody wants to know a colored woman's opinions about her own status or that of her group. When she dares express it, no matter how mild or tactful it may be, it is called "Propaganda," or is labeled "controversial." Those two words have come to have a very ominous sound to me. I cannot escape them; they confront me everywhere I go. (224)

Even in the Progressive era, when politics dominated periodicals, editors could not see activist work on race as aesthetically valuable. Simply because of what Terrell wrote about, she was seen as a propagandist. Her writing and advocacy were so intertwined that she couldn't take well-meaning editors' advice to write about something else; "my whole being was centered on the conditions confronting my race," she explained, "and I poured my very heart's blood into efforts to promote its welfare. It was impossible for me to write on anything which did not concern the race" (230).

In fact, Church mentioned *Uncle Tom's Cabin* as her most important literary model, and wanted to write a Progressive-era version that "depicted the injustice commonly perpetrated upon colored people all over the United States and showed the towering obstacles erected by a cruel race prejudice which they have had to surmount in order to accomplish something worth while ever since they have been emancipated" (233). When she asked two editors if such a "modern *Uncle Tom's Cabin*" could be published, "both Mr. Baker and Mr. Philip Boyden . . . finally admitted that, in their opinion, no periodical in the country would publish any such story at that time" (233). Their judgment, she concluded, "sounded my literary death knell" (233).

African American writers, in other words, had trouble being taken seriously as *writers*. Despite the larger turn toward politically active writing, many periodicals and publishers saw this production as propaganda, not literature. African American writers were constantly drafted to confirm or contradict cultural stereotypes, no matter what their predilections, even if they were deeply invested, as Fauset was, in European high culture. Their race precluded them from being seen as active creators in the larger culture.

The fate of Fauset's black role models bears this out. As Carolyn Sylvander points out, "by 1910 [Paul Laurence] Dunbar was dead (1906), [Charles] Chesnutt was silent, [and Francis E. W.] Harper was eighty-five years old and within a year of her death" (44). Du Bois was still writing, but he was seen primarily as a historian, economist, and activist, not as a writer—and he embraced "propaganda" in ways that Fauset never would, as evidenced by her later pleasure over Boni & Liveright's proclamation that in *There Is Confusion* there was "no propaganda."

Fauset's dilemma was shared by all African American writers at the turn of the century. What is the audience for a black writer? Despite poverty and racial oppression, there was a significant black reading audience. Black colleges in the South, founded during Reconstruction, continued their work despite the violent backlash of Jim Crow, producing educated graduates inspired by Du Bois and the activist work of the NAACP. African American literary societies encouraged literary activity and provided appreciative audiences for writers, particularly black writers. This audience wasn't large and prosperous enough, however, to sustain black writers by themselves. A mixed audience was essential. Fauset couldn't imagine a future as a writer until the twenties, when new possibilities suddenly emerged.

Miscegenation and the New Negro: Negotiation of the Literary Marketplace, 1917–1924

The twenties brought unprecedented publication of African American literature. As James Weldon Johnson observed, Negro fiction received more mainstream attention in the twenties than in all previous periods combined (477). So great was this mainstream interest that Du Bois saw these literary productions as an important front in the NAACP's push for racial equality. David Levering Lewis argues that intervention in the arts "seemed to be the sole battle plan affording both high visibility and low vulnerability. The road to the ballot box and jobs was blocked, but Johnson saw that the door to Carnegie Hall and New York publishers was ajar. Each book, play, poem, or canvas by an Afro-American would become a weapon against the old racial stereotypes" (*When Harlem* 48–49).

That future, however, was significantly different from the one African American Progressives had first imagined. Much has been written about the New Negro ethos, particularly its embrace of the "folk" and its break with the earnest activist of the previous generation, seen as white-identified in the New Negro imagination. Langston Hughes's "The Negro Artist and the Racial Mountain" is the best known of a host of manifestos debunking the theories of the previous generation. Alain Locke's anthology *The New Negro* outlined a new theory of African American identity, forged in urban spaces and centered on a celebratory nativism and nationalism.

The New Negro's emphasis on an innate African American aesthetic consciousness, grounded in a "peasant" class, was an invention—no less an act of self-creation than African American Progressives' creation of humanistic, proud race men and women. It would take another book to investigate the generational hostilities involved in the mutual accusations New Negroes and the older Talented Tenth hurled at each other. Here, I investigate Fauset's complicated relationship with both camps and her own creation of what I call a genteel African American identity.

Fauset came out of a nineteenth-century tradition of uplift, and she made that Christian tradition into a secular vision of art's transformative power. This was not a betrayal of Fauset's black heritage but the means by which she could contribute to the creation of an independent, self-sufficient black culture. Her writings show considerable nuance on this point. In a letter to Du Bois, she stressed the need to "teach our colored men and women *race* pride, *self*-pride, self sufficiency (the right kind), and the necessity of living our lives as nearly as possible, *absolutely*, instead of comparing them always with white standards" (Letter to Du Bois 16 February 1905). Whatever similarities Fauset's program might share with middle-class values were, in her mind, simply incidental, for "the reason we adopt such and such criteria which are also adopted by the Anglo Saxon, is because these criteria are the *best*, and not essentially because they are white." In other words, Fauset felt her combination of middlebrow authorship and progressive, middle-class activism was as black as the blues.

Miscegenation, both racial and cultural, is key to understanding Fauset's notion of African American culture as distinctively American. Fauset knew of African Americans' diversity, in languages, origins, even skin color. She was involved, with Du Bois, in the Pan-African movement, where she met colonial blacks of many languages and nations, and she saw how different black experience was in different parts of the world. African American culture, with its close (if unchosen) interaction with whites, its loss of indigenous African traditions, and its constant influx of black immigrants, was particularly diverse. In her 1929 novel *Plum Bun*, Fauset describes communities in Harlem:

> There sat the most advanced coloured Americans, beautifully dressed, beautifully trained, whimsical, humorous, bitter, impatiently responsible, yet still responsible. In one section loomed the dark, eager faces of West Indians, the formation of their features so markedly different from that of the ordinary American as to give them a wild, slightly feral aspect. . . . Here and there a sprinkling of white faces showed up against a back-ground of patient, softly stolid black faces; faces beaten and fashioned by life into a mold of steady, rock-like endurance, of unshakable, unconquered faith. (*Plum Bun* 216–217)

Fauset's catalog shows the range of black life—humorous, wild, faithful, responsible, even feral—and breaks past the cultural stereotypes that James Weldon Johnson had detailed. The diversity of African American communities was the source of their strength and their beauty. In *Plum Bun*, Fauset uses the fictional Van Meier to ruminate on DuBois's role as spokesman for African American culture, and the source of his genius:

> Of course he doesn't get it from his white blood; he gets it from all his bloods. *It's the mixture that makes him what he is.* Otherwise all white people would be gods. It's the mixture and the endurance which he has learned from being coloured in America and the determination to see life without bitterness. (*Plum Bun* 220–221; italics added)

Miscegenation was the strength and unique genius of African American culture.

This perspective wasn't simply a nineteenth-century literary hold-over but a constant tension in her immediate family. After her mother's death, Fauset's father married a much younger woman who was light-skinned enough to pass. As their son Huff Fauset described the Fauset children, "There were eight of us children, all officially "black." . . . As it was the either of us were almost as distinct from each other, racially speaking, as if we had each come from a different country" (*Autobiography* 148–149). Those who could pass as white were uneducated; Jessie Fauset and her sister Helen, very educated, could not pass. "Confronted with all the hubbub, the guilt and the aura of accusation," Huff Fauset explained, "it was inevitable that the issue of race would extrude in a manner which, for our family, was very unnatural—a manner that rankled in the hearts of all" (76); Jessie and Helen, he claims, were jealous. They "enjoyed the subtle amenities of life, including fine shops, delicacies, intimate theater which white people regardless of class took for granted and Blacks knew were not for them [in America]" (74–75), and they couldn't help but think, "if only *they* had been the ones to be fair-skinned! . . . The treats they could indulge in, if only their skins, like those of their step-siblings, had been lighter by one or two shades!" (76). Fauset's novels of passing, which seemed so contrived and old-fashioned to her contemporaries, derived from her own family's legacy of miscegenation. She thus saw firsthand how irrational racial barriers were, how inessential race was to one's true character and yet how painfully important to the larger culture.

For Fauset, then, Negro essentialism and the racism of white mainstream culture had a similar failing—a disavowal of miscegenation in favor of a fake, and dangerous, doctrine of racial purity. African American culture was both unique *and* intimately connected to the larger American culture; miscegenation allows for both positions. In response to an early accusation that she was white-identified, she wrote a scathing reply:

> Mr. Reuter concludes from my review that "the Negro endeavors to approximate in culture . . . the better standards of American life. . . . If by "better standards," Mr. Reuter means white standards he is greatly mistaken. As I said before the Negro does tend to approximate the appearance of white Americans but that is purely "protective coloring" or rather lack of coloring, sheer adaptation to environment. But the American Negro (including the mulatto) does not try consciously or otherwise to approximate white American culture. He has tried it and found it lacking and he is definitely working out a culture and civilization of his own which while affording many points of contact with white American culture shall yet preserve to him the things which he considers worth while. (Letter to Du Bois 7 April 1919)

Fauset carefully distinguishes "American" and "white." For her, the two are not equivalent; white Americans and American Negroes have equal claim to "American." What one notices in this letter is a tone that Fauset was usually careful to obscure in her public writings. Her telling line, "he has tried [white culture] and found it lacking" shows that America's promise of freedom and equality and the reality of racial discrimination and oppression had made her "bitter," as her brother noted and as she reiterated in an interview in the thirties (Huff Fauset; Jessie Fauset interview in *Southern Workman*). Fauset's genteel literary sensibility, her middle-class ethos, simply appropriated features she was unwilling to abandon simply because white culture also had them ("not white but simply the best"); her ultimate goal, as her work with Du Bois on the *Crisis* attests, was to create an autonomous black culture.

Much to her dismay, American culture in the early twentieth century—including both black and white moderns, apparently—preferred African Americans in blackface. Whether condemning black culture or, as in the twenties, celebrating it, white Americans tended to see the African American community as uniform: primitive, sensual, funny, musical, rhythmic, and simple. They rewarded those who fulfilled their expectations. But even those who worked to embody white expectations did so at a terrible price, as Fauset revealed in a touching tribute to Bert Williams, the famous minstrel performer, who, though black, still performed in blackface:

> If the world knew of his great possibilities why had it doomed this stalwart, handsome creature, to hide his golden skin, his silken hair, his beautiful, sensitive hands under the hideousness of the eternal black make-up. Why should he and we obscure our talents forever under the bushel of prejudice, jealousy, stupidity—whatever it is that makes the white world say: "No genuine colored artist; coons, clowns, end-men, claptrap, but no undisguisedly beautiful presentation of Negro ability." ("The Symbolism of Bert Williams" 14)

For Fauset, stereotypes obscured the true diversity of black culture, and she consistently gravitated toward the one subculture with which she most identified—"cultured," educated African Americans. Locke's nasty comments on this piece—" 'The Gift of Laughter' arrived—and almost provoked tears" show how fraught this definition of black culture was. Locke embraced Williams as the embodiment of New Negro culture.

Black culture, for Fauset, was a conscious creation without the benefit of a documented heritage and past. In her 1921 essay "Nostalgia," she contrasts marginal Americans' quest for a nation, from Greek and Italian immigrants to Jews and "Negroes," and defines African Americans' quest for a "homeland" as idealistic yearning:

> In the main, the American Negro is without ties and the traditions that throw back. Instead, he has built unconsciously from his childhood a dream-country, and yet surely no dream country since it is founded on that document which most realize and sets forth the primal and unchanging needs of man—the Constitution of the United States.
>
> Where the Greek dreams of his statues, he dreams of Justice; where the Italian yearns for his opera, he yearns for Opportunity; and where the Jewish visionary longs for freedom of sect, he cries out for an escape from Peonage.
>
> As a child in his readers, he learns of great principles in the Declaration of Independence, In Fourth of July speeches, in extracts from Daniel Webster, in Mr. Lincoln's Gettysburg address.
>
> He grows up and finds them—not here—just beyond, always beyond; in a country where all things are possible he has found exactly what ought not to be possible. (157)

Fauset imagined black nationhood as a legitimate inflection of American identity that had yet to be realized for African Americans.

Fauset's hostility toward white culture was unsurprising. But it did provide a problem for her development as a writer. Though writers in the Progressive era were able to support themselves from their work in unprecedented numbers, their success depended upon a middle-class audience that was predominantly white. Fauset's ability to imagine that audience, to reach it, to trust it and believe in it, was severely limited by her bitter experiences with racial prejudice. How could she write to a group of people she found "lacking"? How could she imagine a sympathetic relationship with a middlebrow audience?

That problem didn't seem as pressing when Fauset wrote her first novel, in the first flush of the Harlem Renaissance. Nor did the racial essentialism of Negro writers and their white patrons. It would, as I discuss below, recur in the aftermath of *There Is Confusion*'s publication. But at the time of publication, in 1924, all seemed to resolve itself in a moment of possibility.

"A Domestic Allegory of Political Desire": *There Is Confusion*

Fauset had been writing poems, short stories, articles, reviews, and novellas for the *Crisis* for twenty years, reveling in the quasi-private audience of the magazine. The impetus for her entry into more public authorship was T. S. Stribling's *Birthright* (1922), which prompted Fauset, Walter White, and Nella Larsen to begin writing. *Birthright* investigates the African American Peter Siner, "a young, college-educated idealist with messianic tendencies," who wants to reform his Southern hometown (Piacentino 18). Caught tragically between white and black worlds, Siner realizes that each has its own moral structure and is entirely incomprehensible to the other. In the end, he gives up his attempt at assimilation and reform:

> There is no such thing as absolute morals. Morals are as transitory as the sheen on a blackbird's wing; . . . Morals are nothing more than the engines controlling the stream of energy that propel a race on its course. All engines are not alike, nor are all races bound for the same port. Here Peter Siner made the amazing discovery that although he had spent four years in Harvard, he had come out, just as he went in, a negro. (Piacentino 19)

Stribling, in other words, defines whites as innately civilized, educated, and moral, and blacks as sensual, primitive, and instinctive. His cultural relativism and ostensibly sympathetic portrayal of the plight of the educated Negro conceals the most traditional of racial stereotypes. Peter Siner is tragic because his white blood makes him strive for education and culture while his black revolts against such leanings. This racial essentialism would have been most offensive to Fauset. Integration is futile, it says; inequality is perpetual; violent suppression of African Americans is inevitable. Miscegenation, in other words, has not created a new "mixture": "white" blood and "black" blood remained distinct, warring within "mulattos" as black and white did in the larger culture. Reviewers of *Birthright,* to their credit, criticized Stribling for ascribing all of Siner's "negative" qualities to his Negro blood, but none seemed to question the idea that "white" blood and "black" blood were distinct, and were responsible for character. Fed up with the stereotypes that readers took as reality, Fauset proclaimed, "Let us who are better qualified to present [the truth of Negro life] than any white writer, try to do so" (Sylvander 70).

Fauset wrote the novel quickly, though she had been thinking about it, and about its title, for at least a decade (Lewis *W. E. B. Du Bois: Biography* 464). Her *Crisis* connections provided her with key contacts.[3] In fact, for an unpublished writer, she had extraordinary connections with writers and publishers. Alain Locke, before their famous quarrel, was an important resource. Fauset mailed him the manuscript in early 1924 (Letter to Locke 10 January 1923). It isn't entirely clear what she wanted from him. She may have wanted his feedback in revising the manuscript, although in a note attached to it she playfully asks for positive reinforcement: "How nice it is that you are coming! For one thing I can say to you: Didn't you think I did chapter so and so very well indeed? Weren't you pleased with my development of Mr. Oshkosh? No one is so insatiable as your coming author" (Letter to Locke undated). She may have been asking him to put in a good word for her with publishers. Locke seems to have mentioned Jean Toomer to Boni & Liveright, which put out Jean Toomer's *Cane* in 1923 (although Waldo Frank's influence with the firm seems to have been more decisive). It is possible that Locke had a hand in Boni & Liveright's publication of *There Is Confusion* in 1924. No record remains of Locke's response to Fauset's manuscript; from future encounters, one suspects that she was disappointed. Locke didn't ask her to submit either poetry or fiction for *The New Negro*, included her only at Du Bois's insistence and implied threat to abstain, and criticized her for the article she did submit. Whatever Locke's role in the publication of Fauset's first novel, it is clear that she considered him a probable ally. Her imminent, and eventually bitter, estrangement from Locke gave evidence of the gap perceived between "literary merit" and "sentimental propaganda."

As usual, W. E. B. Du Bois was the decisive influence. He read the manuscript and gave editorial advice; his main response was to urge Fauset to be sure not to let the main characters' personal happiness obscure the ongoing struggle for happiness and empowerment of African Americans as a whole. Du Bois's literary agents were Brandt & Brandt; since Fauset also ended up using the agency, it is likely that Du Bois used his influence to make the connection. Brandt & Brandt was a respected New York agency that represented well-known authors Raymond Chandler, e.e. cummings, John Dos Passos, Edna St. Vincent Millay, and Clifford Odets (Bruccoli 287–288). Carl and Zelma Brandt would have handled the placement of Fauset's first novel; after 1926, she would have dealt primarily with Bernice Baumgarten. Baumgarten had an astute sense of the marketplace, and often gave editorial suggestions to her authors. Cozzens's biographer Matthew Bruccoli claims she was known among authors and publishers as "the best agent in New York" (291). Brandt & Brandt successfully placed *There Is Confusion* with Boni & Liveright, which hoped for a best seller and promoted the novel generously.

Fauset's novel was published with great fanfare in April of 1924. The black press generally lauded it as a milestone. A *Pittsburgh Courier* article notes that such economic promotion by a publishing firm for a "colored author" was "unprecedented" (Sylvander 70). One notable advertisement, in the same *New York Times* edition as a review of the novel, highlights the marketing strategy Boni & Liveright employed:

> A Few Weeks Ago—a dinner was given at the Civic Club in New York in honor of Jessie Redmon Fauset which the intellectual leaders of the metropolis attended. They were celebrating the birthday of a new sort of book about colored people—no lynchings, no inferiority complexes, no *propaganda*—the birthday of a fine novel about negroes of the upper classes of New York and Philadelphia—as impressive and vital in their social environment as the upper class

whites whom Edith Wharton or Archibald Marshall love to write about. . . . *Yes there's something new under the sun and it is* **There is Confusion.** (Advertisement for *There Is Confusion*)

For Jessie Fauset, progressive activist and NAACP employee, to be lauded because her novel isn't political and doesn't protest the conditions of African Americans is odd. Even stranger is that Fauset was pleased by this advertisement; she sent it to Langston Hughes with the note, "pretty nice, don't you think?" (Letter to Hughes 28 May 1923). Perhaps the key phrase is "no propaganda"; finally, Fauset may have thought, she had overcome the knee-jerk dismissal of black women's writing of which Mary Church Terrell had complained.

When *There Is Confusion* was published, Fauset must have believed that her literary career was finally secure. She was represented by one of the most successful agencies in New York; she had placed her novel with one of the most prestigious modernist presses, one that published writers like Theodore Dreiser, Ezra Pound, T. S. Eliot, H. L. Mencken, William Faulkner, and Sherwood Anderson. Boni & Liveright had just published Jean Toomer's *Cane (1923)* and seemed committed to developing a market for African American writers. The publication dinner, sponsored by Charles Johnson of *Opportunity,* organized by members of the Saturday Night club, and moderated by Alain Locke, drew Eugene O'Neill, H. L. Mencken, Zona Gale, and Carl Van Vechten (Lewis *W. E. B. Du Bois: The Fight for Equality* 157). Locke gave the novel a favorable review, and by September 1924 it had gone into three American editions with plans for an English and a German edition (Fauset letter to George Douglas Johnson 22 September 1924), selling over two thousand copies (Brandt and Hochman), which seemed a respectable start to a career. Fauset exulted to Langston Hughes, "It is pretty nice to have actually started on what I hope is going to be my life's career and to have the concrete evidence of that beginning" (Letter to Langston Hughes 20 April 1924).

There was trouble on the horizon, however. Having a completed novel, as many struggling writers can attest, did not guarantee her success. *Booklist,* in one of the few unequivocally positive reviews, described *There Is Confusion* as "an earnest treatment of the race problem from a new and interesting angle." That "earnestness" was its primary virtue did not endear it, though, to those for whom middlebrow earnestness was anathema. The *New York Times's* review, for example, claimed that "considered exclusively as fiction, the novel is mediocre: fairly well written, loosely constructed, with most of the usual faults of the propaganda story." The *New Republic* seemed most offended. Its review valued African American literature written "out of his own rich and varied experience, not for the delectation of the whites, but for the edification and enjoyment of his own people," and denounced Fauset's novel as "a work of puny, painstaking labor . . . aimed with unpardonable naiveté at the very young or the pertinently old." That "naiveté" is a key issue; Fauset's reform agenda raised the implicit problem of "propaganda," even as Boni & Liveright's advertising seemed to settle the question.

Younger Harlem Renaissance figures similarly distanced themselves from Fauset's effort. In his published memoirs, Claude McKay defined her writing as "fastidious and precious" as a primrose, and then added a seeming tribute which quickly devolved into a veiled, patronizing insult: "Primroses are pretty. I remember the primroses where I live in Morocco, that lovely melancholy land of autumn and summer and mysterious veiled brown women. When the primroses spread themselves across the barren hillsides before the sudden summer blazed over the hot land, I often thought of Jessie Fauset and her novels" (quoted in Sylvander 62). Privately, though, McKay wasn't nearly so whimsical. In a letter to Josephine Herbst in 1924, he lambasted the book for the apparently mutually exclusive transgressions of kowtowing to whites and being a Talented Tenth self-help book.

> About that Confusion book I thought it awfully written—no attention to plot and bringing out of details, quite a confusion in itself. But I never could see what Jessie was driving at though I tried to read it twice. Seems to me her chief purpose is to show the whites that there is an exclusive upper ten of Negroes and how they live. The writer is typical of that clan of coloured people. . . . They are awful people and you'll find the type in every subject race. But worst of it is that among American Negroes they are the practically the *only* articulate ones and they have behind them that awful gang of New England and Quaker philanthropists—the people that read the "Nation."
>
> On the other hand, I don't think Jessie wanted to show the white characters as *bad*. She is writing a Sunday school self help tract for good behaving Negroes and it works out that way. . . . She has no perspective, no social, psychological, not even a humanitarian out-

> look on the Negro question. I don't think she *feels* even—for instance she makes Joanna an *artist* while her reactions to life around her are precisely those of a clod-hopper! . . .
>
> I don't use my facts (at least I try not to) for propaganda value. For me the facts are not final entities by themselves, but atmosphere against whose lights and shades move my characters in whom I am much more interested as people. (Letter to Herbst 18 August 1924)

In McKay's sweeping condemnation of *There Is Confusion,* all the seeds of Fauset's later critical disfavor are evident—her sycophancy to condescending whites; her faith in uplift and progress; her propagandistic preference for types instead of developed character; her "bad writing." McKay's literary aesthetic, his dismissal of middle-class African Americans as "awful people," and his radical impatience with liberalism (in the same letter, he assures Herbst that "the root of the race trouble in America is entirely economic" and so simple race relations are passé), make *There Is Confusion* unintelligible to him. He spends most of his letter imagining pernicious and contradictory motives on the basis not of what Fauset wrote but of who she was—a middle-class Progressive, a member of the Talented Tenth and the Philadelphia elite, and hence, the enemy.

The paradigm of domestic political authorship, however, reveals a very different novel. *There Is Confusion* skillfully balances subversion and assimilation, to critique American racism from within an American mainstream. Formally, Fauset's novel is a hybrid of at least two forms: the sentimental novel, with dramatic story lines, polemic speeches, and resolution of conflict in marriage; and the realistic novel (perhaps best represented by *A Hazard of New Fortunes*), with its neutral, unsparing narrative voice and its interweaving of widely divergent social strata. The novel appeals to emotion through vivid descriptions of Joanna and Peter's separation and reunion, the anguish of Maggie's failed marriage and thwarted dreams of love, and the tragedy of World War I casualties. Fauset's story contains various love triangles, a dramatic jealous stabbing, and Meriwether Bye's suicidal renunciation of life and privilege. Through sentimental conventions, Fauset is able to satisfy her audience's desire for a moral with occasional discussions of race. *There Is Confusion* embeds its polemics in conversations.

The novel's realistic technique allows the author to subtly critique each character's viewpoint without advocating any one as correct. No character can speak for Fauset: Joanna, the ostensible heroine, is dogmatic and snobby; Peter is lazy and flighty; Maggie is dependent on social respectability and male validation. All the characters are flawed. Fauset is also able to depict the influence of racism, not just on a small group of African Americans, but on American society at large. Old-money white Americans, upper-middle-class blacks, lower-class blacks, theater owners, medical students, musicians—her characters, skillfully interwoven, represent American society as a whole.

There Is Confusion provides a Progressive history of African Americans from the early 1900s till the end of World War I, and reframes the Harlem Renaissance in political terms. African American culture and arts are seen to involve a desire for greatness, for influence, for fame, and for equality. The novel thus goes against the grain of what Du Bois termed a newly emergent "defeatist genre of Negro art, which is so common and at the present apparently inescapable" (quoted in Sylvander 17–18). "The time has come," he insisted, "for the Negro to be treated humanly . . . not only as to his suffering, but as to his plain and unquestionable triumphs" (18). Fauset's novel reveals an undeniable faith in progress, activism, and effort in her attempt to highlight these triumphs.

The novel begins and ends with the quest for greatness, which is intimately bound with power. The young Joanna Marshall, like her father, Joel, longs for distinction and seeks models. He tutors her (and both white and black readers) in African American history and achievement, teaching her about great people like "Douglass and Vesey and Turner . . . Harriet Tubman, Phillis Wheatley, Sojourner" (14); his own tastes run to leaders like Napoleon, Lincoln, Garrison, Frederick Douglass, and Toussaint L'Ouverture. Political leaders, reformers, and revolutionists, black and white, lay equal claim to what the novel defines as "greatness"; what matters most is that one's achievements transform, in some way, the social fabric of the nation.

Progress thus determines whether one is truly great, and progress, as a people and as a nation, is the obsession of most of the black characters in *There Is Confusion*. Joel, the patriarch of the Marshall family, is "obsessed with the idea of a progressing younger generation" (68). Advancement is their goal, and with optimism, Joel's children are convinced that they can progress beyond racial prejudice; by connecting the ideas of progress and racial equality, Fauset can convert her white readers to equality and her black readers to progress. Joanna, in her relentless insistence on fame and recognition in the public sphere, is the main spokesperson for "Negro" progressivism:

> Colored people . . . can do everything that anybody else can do. They've already done it. Some one colored person somewhere in the world does as good a job as anyone else, —perhaps a better one. They've been kings and queens and poets and teachers and doctors and everything. I'm going to be the one colored person who sings best in these days, and I never, never, never mean to let color interfere with anything I *really* want to do. (45)

What Joanna wants is evident in her quest for recognition in the arts, and in her brother Philip's creation of a civil rights organization for the benefit of the race and of the country as a whole (a fictionalized NAACP provided for white readers). It is further embedded in the histories of Fauset's characters, which provide a Progressive version of how African Americans have risen "up from slavery." Peter Bye is finally converted to the Progressive faith through Joanna's example and through his own family history. His grandfather founded a school that educated ex-slaves, and carefully recorded family history to demonstrate that his family were "people of importance." Peter reads the creed of uplift in his grandfather's picture: " 'I have made the most of myself,' the proud old face seemed to say. 'My father was a slave, but I am a teacher, a leader of men' " (186). Upward mobility is the only religion of note evident in *There Is Confusion*. The Marshalls attend church Sunday for every conceivable reason—the mother for propriety, Joanna for singing, Philip for rhetorical tutelage, Sylvia to display her wardrobe—*except* religious sentiment. But the quest for distinction more than amply compensates for their missing faith.

For all of its characters, both working and upper class, *There Is Confusion* rewards effort and education with success, and laziness and slothfulness with poverty. Peter's problems come from his father Meriwether, who "through sickness, gambling, and a hitherto unsuspected penchant for sheer laziness" succeeded in "wiping away all that edifice of respectability and good citizenship which Isaiah Bye had so carefully built up" (31). His false creed is that "if life has any favors for you, she'll give them to you without your asking for them. The world owes you a living, let it come to you, don't bother going after it" (33). This apostasy is resoundingly refuted throughout the novel.

The true religion of middle-class values is found not only in education and a work ethic, but also in the arts. Joanna's quest for greatness shifts almost imperceptibly from the political to the cultural sphere. Pragmatism, however, convinces Joel Marshall that shifting patterns in the culture may permit Joanna to make culture the basis of reform:

> "Nothing in reason," he used to tell Joanna, "is impossible. . . . Ten years ago people would have laughed at the thought of colored people on the stage. Look at the bill-boards on Broadway."
>
> It was in the first part of the century when Williams and Walker, Cole and Johnson, Ada Overton and others were at their zenith. Old Joel believed them the precursors of greater things. Since Joanna's gifts were those of singing and dancing, he hoped to make her famous the country over. Of course he would have preferred a more serious form of endowment. But such as it was, it was Joanna's, and must be developed. Joel Marshall believed in using the gifts nearest at hand. (18)

In building a black middlebrow culture, however, the arts have even greater potential than Joel Marshall imagines. "Colored art" could transform America. The emerging Harlem Renaissance is thus political.

The arts are can be politically effective because through art Joanna can establish African Americans' humanity and American-ness. She explains to her brother-in-law, "I want to show *us* to the world. I am colored, of course, but American first. Why shouldn't I speak to all America?" (76). The arts are especially effective because emotional experience can establish the essential similarities among ethnic groups. Joanna finds, for example, that music can make people forget color. At a concert, she says, "Did you see that white woman next to me edge away when I sat down? But when she heard me humming after it was over, she leaned over and asked me if I knew the words" (77). The arts have already brought Joanna an understanding of Europeans, evidenced by her commitment to German Romantic poets like Goethe. Greenwich Village radicals eventually give her a chance on the stage, using their culture to overcome prejudice. Vera Sharples, a white radical, insists that "art to my eye is art, and there's no sense in letting a foolish prejudice interfere with it" (227). Education, hard work, and culture are the crucial components of the middlebrow program in *There Is Confusion*.

Fauset takes pains to avoid identifying this program solely with middle-class characters, however. Maggie Ellersley, a child of awful poverty, shows how effective this gospel of uplift is for the lower classes. The daughter of "a spare hard-working woman to whom life had meant nothing but poverty and confusion" (55), Maggie has revolted against the "sordidness" of the Tenderloin district and devised a plan for escape, which involves a boarding house in a more decent neighborhood. Thus she gets "her first insight into the workings of life. If you wanted things, you thought and thought about them, and when an opportunity offered, there you were with your mind made up to jump at it" (62). Maggie is consistently praised for her rise from slum child to successful businesswoman, while other middle-class characters, like Joanna, are condemned for despising her. Maggie's main flaw (and all the characters have a flaw they must correct) is her desire for respectability for its own sake, a quest she atones for at the end of the novel (268). Fauset's Progressive agenda, in other words, is intended not just for the benefit of the Talented Tenth but for all African Americans.

Of course, the novel is not as inclusive of working-class African Americans as Fauset probably would have claimed. *There Is Confusion* occasionally associates respectability and progress not with character qualities but with material possessions and comfort. Peter Bye's aunt, for example, recognizes the Marshalls' superiority as much through their proper furniture as through their "spirit . . . of ambition and hopefulness": "She liked Joel's success, his pride, his air of being somebody. She estimated rightly the correctness of the old-fashioned walnut furniture, the heavy curtains, the kidney table in the parlor, the massive service and good linen" (51). This fetishizing of the material runs counter to Fauset's contention that it is character, not class, that determines progress and uplift. Joanna avers that "I do care about success. And a house or a car usually implies that" (110). Susan Tomlinson argues that Fauset's focus on material goods is a critique, not a celebration, of middle-class materialism (235). Yet Fauset's emphasis on material respectability, like the advertisements for such goods in women's magazines, is problematic for an egalitarian black culture.

A fastidious distaste for black English further limits the potential universal appeal of Fauset's independent black culture. Only lower-class characters speak in dialect, and it is a dialect that lessens their dignity. Maggie, for example, has her "calla-lily charm visibly lessened . . . when she opened her pretty mouth," because her slangy response to would-be suitors is "aw quit your kidding!" (58). And unlike Langston Hughes and Zora Neale Hurston, who incorporated black English into literary genres, Fauset refuses to consider this dialect anything but "incorrect English." She refers to gambler Neale Henderson's speech on more than one occasion as "deliberately incorrect," and the way he talks is the strongest symbol of his antisocial violence; only a man who spoke with "deliberate incorrectness" would be capable of the stabbing he later commits. Fauset's rejection of black English as a legitimate part of African American culture further calls her vision of an independent black culture into question for lower-class and Southern blacks.

These apparent class biases may indicate that when Fauset insisted that her work must stand and fall by her black audience, she meant a black middle-class audience. Her very blindness to black folk culture could recommend her writing to a middle-class, mixed audience suspicious of free sexuality. Certainly, Fauset used her writing to educate white Americans about the anti-American "confusion" of racism. Her main characters have the assumed values and even the prejudices of white, middle-class America; white middle-class readers are thus guided toward the main characters' insights and critiques. When Joanna, filled with self-righteous zeal and the Puritan work ethic, proclaims that race prejudice is "an awful nuisance; in some parts of this country it is more than a nuisance, it's a veritable menace" (98), or realizes "how completely colored Americans were mere on-lookers at the possibilities of life" (235), readers may believe her because she speaks in familiar language.

Fauset further uses her story, and specifically the character of Peter Bye, to challenge the stereotype of the tragic mulatto. In traditional formulations, mulattoes suffer because they are both rational, from their "white" blood, and corrupt, from their "black" blood. This "wisdom" is challenged by the Bye family, white and black, who are uncannily similar. As Peter notes when he first goes to the white Bye home,

> I wish you could have seen that old butler, Janna. He knew my grandfather. And the moment he saw me, he knew I was a Bye. Gave me the funniest look. "Why," he said, "you'se the spit of both families!" Funny, isn't it, Joanna; those two families, the black and the white Byes, lived so long together that they developed similar characteristics, like husbands and wives, you know. And they say white and colored people are fathoms apart!" (280–281)

It turns out, of course, that the similarity of the black and white Byes isn't just conditioning. Mixed-blood Peter Bye is lazy and shiftless because of his white heritage, not his black. Upon learning that the white Philadelphia Byes are also his ancestors, he says to his wife, "See, dear, there is the source of all I used to be. My ingratitude, my inability to adopt responsibility, my very irresoluteness come from that strain of white Bye blood. But I understand it now, I can fight against it. I'm free, Joanna, free" (297). Fauset thus inverts the stereotype of the mulatto.

Through the mulatto figure, Fauset can also highlight miscegenation: not only culturally but racially, it is the rule. Equality does not produce miscegenation; it is, in fact, the inequality of America that has resulted in racial mixing, a mixing that makes obvious white guilt and betrayal. Fauset thus claims for her characters a central and assimilated, not marginal, American identity.

This focus on American identity is crucial to Fauset's middlebrow approach. Peter Bye descends from the distinguished Bye family of Philadelphia, the birthplace of America; a black character is thus a "blueblood" American. Accused of forsaking her Negro heritage, Joanna says, "You don't think I want to forsake—*us*. Not at all. But I want to show us to the world. I am colored, of course, but American first. Why shouldn't I speak to all America?" (76). In Joanna's triumphant dance representing America, she wears a mask. After her performance, the audience demands that she pull off her mask and show the face of America. Unlike Bert Williams, Joanna is both willing and able to do so:

> There was a moment's silence, a moment's tenseness. Then Joanna smiled and spoke. "I hardly need to tell you that there is no one in the audience more American than I am. My great-grandfather fought in the Revolution, my uncle fought in the Civil War and my brother is 'over there' now." . . .
>
> The tightly packed audience took up the applause again and Joanna was a star. (232)

Through scenes like these, Fauset contests definitions of American history that exclude her. Her place is within American history, identity, and values.

This claim is made as much for her black readers as for her white. Though Fauset wanted to persuade white readers, her primary aim was an inclusive black middlebrow culture. She ends the novel, against the backdrop of World War I, having proposed a "greatness" that includes every hardworking African American family. Having shown single women working at independent careers, Fauset concludes her novel with marriage and family.

After establishing a progressive matrix for the Harlem Renaissance, Fauset resolves her characters' struggles through a traditional family, as Frances Harper did before her. Joanna finds success hollow; her fame may "be shared with any girl who chose to stick feathers, Indian fashion, in her hat. An empty thing—different, so different from what she had expected it to be" (270). When she demands to know whether her success was her father's "idea of real greatness," he tells her "that he, too, had hoped for something different" (236). It does not affect the country at large; Southern newspapers reject the claim of a "Negress" to represent America. She longs to do "something useful" (270). That "usefulness" comes through marriage to Peter Bye, in which she subordinates her own career to his, following the "black Madonna" model of female uplift emphasized by the Talented Tenth.

Joanna's brother Philip must also rethink his dreams of greatness in politics. He rejects happiness with the lower-class Maggie for the glory of the battlefield. Recovering from war wounds, Philip confesses his wrong to Maggie, but places the blame not on himself but on America's racial prejudice:

> Now as I look back, I think I realize for the first time what this awful business of color in America does to a man, what it has done for me. If we weren't so persistently persecuted and harassed that we can think, breathe, do nothing but consider our great obsession, you and I might have been happy long ago. (266–267)

Obsessing on difference and neglecting common human concerns, Fauset argues, is as wrong as doing nothing—and as much a triumph for the forces of racist confusion. The middle-class work ethic, in the end, must be as moderate as anything else.

Fauset's solution for both of these couples—Peter and Joanna, Philip and Maggie—is "greatness, even in daily living" (297). Their greatness comes from very ordinary concerns of marriage and family. Maggie gives up her quest for respectability, and Joanna gives up her career; marital happiness and the education of children is the most important sign of progress for African Americans. In its conclusion, *There Is Confusion* most reflects the influence of Frances Harper's *Iola Leroy.* Love is the great salvation; when Maggie and Philip finally find each other—with Philip exclaiming, "Oh, my little yellow flower, I'll never let you go"—Fauset transforms a Christian symbol into a more universal sign of faith and love: "Outside, the cross on Nivrolet, a luminous symbol of faith, pointed steadfastly to heaven" (268). And Joanna learns to replace her personal ambition with a racial ambition centered on her husband:

> Perhaps it is wrong to imply that Joanna had lost her ambition. She was still ambitious, only the field of her ambition lay without herself. It was Peter now whom she wished to see succeed. . . . In a thousand little ways she deferred to him, and showed him that as a matter of course he was the arbiter of her own and her child's destiny, the *fons et origo* of authority. So he grew both in the spirit of racial tolerance and in the spirit of responsibility. (292)

Romantic love and family responsibility, then, become the marks of greatness, which anyone with feeling and determination can achieve. Fauset's egalitarian middlebrow culture turns away from feminism and cultural radicalism toward individual happiness; cultural transformation comes through the family, controlled and guided by women. The harbinger of greatness is love. Joanna proclaims, "I learned that nothing in the world is worth as much as love. For people like us, people who can and must suffer—*Love* is our refuge and strength" (283–284). Fauset's story of the Harlem Renaissance connects African American culture in the twenties with its its roots in nineteenth-century reform, social gospel, and republican motherhood; it was perfectly attuned to the Talented Tenth audience.

Miscegenating Middlebrow and the Limits of Identification

After a promising beginning to her authorial career, nothing went smoothly for Fauset. Boni & Liveright, despite sales that were certainly no worse than those of other writers under contract, declined her second novel. She spent several years trying to place this book, *Plum Bun,* calling in favors from everyone, even Carl Van Vechten, whom she viewed with great ambivalence, if not outright suspicion.

Her agent seemed unenthusiastic about her work. Though Brandt & Brandt placed her first and second novels, Bernice Baumgarten seems to have been neither friend nor advocate. By the 1950s, when she contacted them to try to sell her last two novels to the movies,Brandt and Brandt had forgotten that they had ever represented her (Letter to Langston Hughes 2 October 1950). The agency didn't seem to believe in her work, as they did in the work of other clients with modest sales, nor in her future as a writer. If they had originally taken her only at Du Bois's suggestion, they may have resented the obligation. The warmth that existed between Dorothy Canfield and Paul Reynolds, Pearl Buck and David Lloyd, even Herbst and Maxim Lieber (and Herbst was, if anything, less successful in the marketplace than Fauset) is absent in Fauset's relationship with her agent. Their correspondence hasn't survived, but that in itself may be telling.

Brandt & Brandt eventually placed *Plum Bun* with the British publisher Charles Elkin Mathews in 1928, and ended their professional relationship with her (Brandt and Hochman). How Fauset found her second American publisher, Frederick A. Stokes, is unclear. Stokes may have had a relationship with the British firm, or the popular Progressive writer Zona Gale may have had some influence. Fauset's relationship with Stokes had its own problems. Before Stokes would agree to publish *The Chinaberry Tree* (the next book after *Plum Bun*), the firm insisted on a preface by Gale to testify to the story's authenticity. Gale assured readers that there really were "cultured" Negroes like those Fauset describes. Fauset, in a letter graciously thanking Gale, a longtime NAACP supporter, for her preface, added wryly, "the joke of it is that the people in my story don't begin to measure up to the capable and efficient colored women you've been meeting at conventions. They are just decent, ambitious folks with sensibilities. Yes—their like is unknown" (Letter to Zona Gale 22 October 1931). Depending upon white patronage to authenticate the truth of her story, as if she were publishing a slave narrative in the 1850s, must have been deeply humiliating. Fauset wasn't happy with what she saw as her publishers' neglect; in 1954, she complained to Langston Hughes that Lippincott, which bought out Stokes after its bankruptcy, had done nothing to promote her novels, which were still selling after twenty years despite the utter lack of advertising (Letter to Hughes 2 October 2 1950).

Fauset's two publishers seemed lukewarm, at best, and she had to struggle with both to tell the stories she wanted to tell. Neither seemed to offer very good advice on how to develop the audience she needed. In short, Fauset didn't have the command of the market that Canfield and Buck did—or even Herbst, who despite her marginality as a radical had a devoted agent and contacts within presses. Fauset's relationships with publishers and agents were difficult and ultimately disappointing.

Many Harlem Renaissance writers complained of their relationships with publishers, particularly about how opportunities vanished with the onset of the Depression and the next "new" thing, proletarian literature. Race is central to the issue, but publishers' relationships with black writers involved more than simple racism. Most writers in the twenties complained of publishers' neglect, materialism, and philistinism; the laments of Harlem Renaissance writers must be seen in a broader context.

Publishers needed an angle, a niche, for marketing; they placed writers within an existing "school," or created one their writer could epitomize. In the twenties, publishers marketed black writers as an offshoot of the "modern youth rebellion," which confronted middle-class culture and offended conventional sensibilities. The Negro became a symbol of everything the radicals felt was missing from American life. To fit into this market niche, a writer must show the essence of "true" blackness rather than derivative culture. For writers who fulfilled this role—Langston Hughes, Zora Neale Hurston, Claude McKay—there were publishing contracts, critical acclaim, and valuable networking with Greenwich Village moderns. This doesn't mean that such writers of the "folk" were only fulfilling white expectations, but that they were able to use a publishing trend to articulate their own vision of African American culture.

In other words, the Harlem Renaissance both made Jessie Fauset's career and relegated her to marginal status within it. Publishers interested in cultural rebellion saw African American writers as potentially valuable in the market for urban white readers. But publishers who made the mistake of thinking that all black writers were cultural rebels, like Boni & Liveright, were quickly disabused of that notion.

It is hard to think of a press less suited to Jessie Fauset than Boni & Liveright. Horace Liveright delighted in offending middle-class sensibilities and flaunting its conventions; his office was famous for its free flow of liquor and its revolving cast of Broadway beauties. Liveright seemed to like nothing better than a big obscenity case, and fought for Theodore Dreiser with relish (Dardis 75–76). Dignified, middle-class Jessie Fauset could not have been more out of place.

On the other hand, Fauset's writing seems perfectly geared to the women's magazine audience with which Canfield, and later Buck, connected. A publication like the *Woman's Home Companion* had articles against lynching and stories that contained pleas for racial equality, like *The Brimming Cup.* These magazines also paid well; one serialized novel could have supported Fauset for years. Fauset often asked friends about the fees other magazines, like *Opportunity,* paid. She was desperate to quit teaching and make a living solely from her writing; she told the *Southern Workman* of reading popular magazines to try to figure out the "germ" of popular writing (Starkey 217). She wrote to Langston Hughes, "How much I'd like to write a best seller! Everything then would be feasting and fun" (Letter 23 September 1925). Fauset had professional contact with writers who wrote for these magazines, including Zona Gale, Dorothy Canfield, and Pearl Buck, and their intervention could have made a difference. Women's magazines would seem to have been the right platform for Fauset's style and themes; her novels seem more at home with the novels serialized in women's magazines than they do when read against Zora Neale Hurston or Jean Toomer.

And yet, I cannot see find any evidence that she submitted her work to women's magazines. Nor can I find any evidence that she tried to use her literary agents to place any writing with those magazines. Admittedly, her publishing records have largely been lost, but the existing records of Brandt & Brandt indicate that she tried to place work only with publishing houses, not magazines (Brandt and Hochman). She seems to have written only novels after the publication of *There Is Confusion;* the short stories and novellas she wrote for the *Crisis* seem to be early treatments for plots in her later novels. Nor have I found any evidence that she corresponded with Canfield and Buck for literary advice. The saved correspondence with Zona Gale was only about Gale's preface for her novel.

This lack of evidence is mysterious, given Fauset's aesthetic and literary aims and her desire for financial solvency. Of course, it may be that she tried these magazines and was rejected, and the records simply haven't been kept. She may not have had a choice about where to be published. No black writers were published in women's magazines in the twenties and thirties, at least none that I have found. No black writers were published by the Book-of-the-Month Club until 1939, and then the novel wasn't one concerning the Talented Tenth but the shocking tale of the lower-class murderer Bigger Thomas, in Richard Wright's *Native Son.* Middlebrow readers may have been exposed to writing about African Americans, even to writing that advocated for them, but they didn't embrace, or didn't have access to, African Americans depicted as one of "us." However miscegenated actual American culture might be, middlebrow readers inhabited a fictional land of Jim Crow.

Racial exclusion doesn't entirely answer the question, however; it seems unlikely that Fauset wouldn't submit writing to women's magazines because she assumed that they wouldn't accept her. The NAACP challenged racial restrictions as its core work, and much of Fauset's identity as a writer involved challenging common assumptions about the black community and authorship. A lack of precedent wouldn't have intimidated her; as for discouragement, Fauset seems to have been doggedly persistent about her writing all her life. Du Bois paid her a somewhat backhanded compliment (considering that the end of their relationship sent Fauset out of New York's literary atmosphere and into exile in an unhappy marriage in New Jersey) when he praised her willingness to "peg away utterly oblivious to mere matters of money and applause" (Letter to Fauset 25 September 1934). Yet she doesn't seem to have even tried women's magazines.

Perhaps, hoping to free herself from association with "propaganda," Fauset didn't want to also take on the burden of "trash." Women's magazines had no cultural capital; writers like Canfield who chose to write there did so for access to audience and for pay, not for reputation. Fauset had already borne misogyny from African American critics. She wrote to Langston Hughes years later, in 1949, after another slight from the critic Arna Bontemps, "I've suffered a good deal from colored men writers from Locke down to Bontemps—you know 'Without sneering teach the rest to sneer,' sort of thing" (Letter to Hughes 9 June 1949). African American male critics participated in a general backlash against women's writing; Locke's complicity may have been owing in part to a casual misogyny that many of the gay Harlem Renaissance writers shared; small wonder that Fauset's middle-class culture, grounded in republican motherhood and the "feminine," should be consistently devalued by them. By scapegoating black women like Fauset, these critics could prove their manhood. Fauset's letter to Locke demonstrates how aesthetic criteria (which she repeatedly refers to as ill-defined and arbitrary) are often a cover for complicated race and gender politics.

Whatever the reasons, Jessie Fauset didn't gain access to the mixed audiences necessary for financial success. She wrote no more novels after 1934. But she never stopped hoping that her novels could reach a mainstream audience and help broaden the national conversation on race. In 1950, she wrote Langston Hughes for help in getting some of her novels made into films, for "this wave of movies about colored people has made me eager to get my own books before the producers" (Letter to Hughes 22 October 1949). Her attempts to find an agent and introduce her novels to even larger audiences through movies also, unfortunately, failed. Fauset, in the end, was primarily a writer of the black middle class in the interwar period, and identified herself as such. She was pleased, she wrote at the time, by "favorable comments from *colored people* everywhere," by whose "judgment the book must stand or fall" (Letter to Langston Hughes 20 April 1924). But literate African Americans could not sustain a novelist at the time. It wasn't until the 1970s that African American reading communities, supplemented by (mainly) white women readers, supported writers like Alice Walker, Gloria Naylor, and Toni Morrison, and more recently Terry McMillan. Fauset thought about how to build "a colored market," consulting with the book collector Jesse Moorland about creating "a campaign for my book so it will go off with a rush which will be heartening to the publishers and will mean something to future writers" (Letter to Jesse Moorland 26 March 1934). Later writers benefited from second wave feminism and Oprah's Book Club. But all this was many years too late for Fauset.

Elizabeth McHenry suggests that the Saturday Nighters was the community of readers that fostered Jean Toomer's *Cane* (267). In many ways, though, Fauset's later fiction better matched the desires and preferences of this educated black middle-class audience. Her symbiotic relationship with educated African American readers, people with similar political and cultural outlooks, marks her as that rarest of artists in the interwar period—a black middlebrow writer.

THREE

Multicultural Middlebrow

Pearl Buck and the Liberal Iconography of The Good Earth

On 3 August 1932, two hundred people, the cream of New York's literary world, gathered at the new Waldorf-Astoria to honor the elusive author of an unexpected best seller—*The Good Earth.* The novel, by a relatively unknown missionary living in China, had leapt into the national consciousness (and put its publisher, John Day, into sudden solvency) when the Book-of-the-Month Club selected it in March 1931. Dorothy Canfield, who read the novel on the train back to Vermont from a monthly BOMC meeting, persuaded her fellow judges through her spirited advocacy (Conn 123). From there, the novel kept selling, captivating middle-class readers with its inside view of China; as one prominent advertisement put it, *The Good Earth* "drew aside the veil" to show the innate kinship of the Chinese and middle-class Americans.

In a rare convergence, *The Good Earth* was also embraced by modern writers and critics who sensed in the as yet unseen author a kindred spirit. After *The Good Earth* was published, many reviewers praised its frankness about sex, its unsentimental tone, and its insight into a complex culture. "Common humanity," in the author's lexicon, was sensual, instinctive, kind and cruel by impulse, and deeply connected with the rhythms of the earth.

Buck's personal life also made her seem in sympathy with cultural rebellion. Shortly after the Waldorf-Astoria dinner, Buck reported to the Presbyterian mission board and publicly criticized missionary work as arrogant and imperialist, precipitating her resignation from the board. Buck biographer Peter Conn has compared the furor over her "Is There a Case for Foreign Missions?" with the Scopes "monkey trial" (151), seen by moderns as a salvo against American religious superstition. Buck's affair with her publisher, Richard Walsh, would become public knowledge in 1935, when the *New York Times* reported her Reno divorce and her marriage, within the hour, to Walsh (a union demonstrating not only Buck's sexual liberation, but also her financial acumen). Most titillating to the tabloids was the fact that Buck and Walsh's soon-to-be ex-wife, Ruby Walsh, had traveled to Reno together and "shared lodgings throughout the six weeks required by Nevada law to establish their local residence" (Conn 182). By having her sex life advertised in the papers, Buck joined a small but distinguished group of cultural rebels.

Perhaps just as important, Buck seemed to know her place. At that same Waldorf-Astoria dinner, she denigrated the role of the novelist, drawing on a Chinese literary tradition that refused to view it as literature. As Alexander Woollcott described the address, Buck "told us all that, throughout the greater part of Chinese history, novelists had been regarded as such negligible creatures that they were ignored by their contemporaries and handed on nameless to posterity. One gathered that she was beginning to think it a good idea" (22). In her own memoir, written twenty years later, she recalled quoting from the Chinese novelist Shi-Naian: "How can I know what those who come after me and read my book will think of it? I cannot even know what I, myself, born into another incarnation, will think of it. I do not know if I, myself, afterwards can even read this book. Why therefore would I care?" (*My Several Worlds* 76).

Woollcott noted her lack of pretension approvingly. Buck, "inexpert as a speaker and obviously bewildered by the curious gentry around her, . . . read aloud a lovely old fabric of miraculously apposite Chinese prose transmuted with a cadence which is half the secret of her alchemy" (22). He placed Buck's "inexpert" performance in stark contrast with the "odd mixture of belles letters and ballyhoo" that corrupts literature. Buck's humility at that banquet, critics seemed to think, made her safe to praise.

Considering what was to come—Buck's embrace of women's magazines and liberal activism, her vilification by these same critics after her

1938 Nobel Prize, her enthusiastic self-promotion, and her postwar dismissal as a publicity-seeking women's novelist—it is tempting to linger over this literary banquet. Because Buck hadn't yet been labeled, the event mixed a diverse group of writers and critics. Popular writers Fannie Hurst and Christopher Morley rubbed shoulders with Alexander Woollcott and with Harold Ross of the *New Yorker;* upstart publishers Richard Simon and Max Schuster mingled with industry elder Henry Holt and BOMC president Harry Scherman, and with Henry Seidel Canby, a BOMC judge and middlebrow critic. Historians, academics, cartoonists, and newspaper editors, including the conservative Henry Luce, "the young publisher of *Time* and another child of Presbyterian missionaries in China" (Conn 145)—all were there, in some sense, to lay claim to Buck.

It turned out, of course, that Woollcott and the other cultural rebels misjudged Buck profoundly. By their standards, her authorial identity was inscrutable, a mix of liberal activism, plot-driven narratives, and self-righteous self-promotion. Even Peter Conn, in a sympathetic and thoroughly researched biography, ends by admitting that he cannot "pierce the veil of mystery and accident that led the daughter of pious missionaries on a journey from obscurity and poverty to world fame and a lifelong campaign for justice" (381). But where Pearl Buck becomes comprehensible is at the intersection of progressivism, women's novels, and middlebrow authorship.

American Dreams, Chinese Realities: Construction of Authorship

China had long been a symbol of the exotic other in American culture, an inferior, backward country that needed Christianity and capitalism (Leong 7). American writers, notably Ezra Pound, used "the Orient" as a metaphor—for vice, for sex, for the primitive—but always for strangeness and otherness. For Pearl Buck, however, China was not an exotic metaphor but a daily, material reality. The daughter of Christian missionaries, she had spent all but one year of her childhood in China. Her four-year tenure at Randolph-Macon Women's College, which exposed her to feminist role models like Anna Louise Strong, didn't affect her connection with China; after graduation, she returned, married, and lived there until she was nearly forty years old. Leong finds, in Buck's early letters as a new missionary, evidence of orientalist, colonialist attitudes. As she shed her Christian fundamentalism, however, Buck's identification with the Chinese increased. She proclaimed in 1933, "By birth and ancestry I am American; by choice and belief I am a Christian; but by the years of my life, by sympathy and feeling, I am Chinese" (*My Several Worlds* 155). These identifications stem from her cross-cultural exposure to stories; her claim to Chinese identity demonstrates a Deweyan faith in the power of writing to bridge cultural divides.

Buck's writing education came not from formal schooling (she was home-schooled by her mother) but through an eclectic range of influences: classics of genteel culture, popular magazines, missionary publications, Confucian texts, Chinese storytelling and popular novels. Two identifications were primary: an imaginary and simplified Western concept of the great author, and the popular and anonymous Chinese vernacular tradition.

Pearl Buck learned about Western authorship primarily through books her parents owned or that she was able to buy from Kelly and Walsh, an English bookstore in Shanghai (*My Several Worlds* 62). Her parents owned the holy texts of genteel culture: "sets of Dickens and Thackeray and George Eliot and Walter Scott and their company, and we had the English poets and a fine edition of Shakespeare, and these were a solid part of my childhood" (62–63). Dickens was a particular favorite, and an important precursor to the kind of writer Buck would become—he was episodic, plot-driven, emotional, and firmly grounded in contemporary political and social issues. Buck wrote of Dickens exercising his "usual influence . . . to stir alive the young imagination and create wonder about human beings" (75). Her mother worried about his coarse appeal to the lower classes (75), although for Buck, this popular reach was part of his appeal, and connected the English tradition with the Chinese vernacular. Like the illiterate despot, Mr. Todd, in Evelyn Waugh's *A Handful of Dust*, she read Dickens completely through every year.

Dickens probably appealed to Buck because he was the populist in the group. The English writers in her bound set were safely canonized, culturally significant, "universal"—safe for missionaries abroad. Dickens was "coarse," just as the Chinese popular traditions Buck would embrace were unpretentious, earthy, and popular. And yet, despite her preference for Dickens, Buck took in the lessons of the genteel canon. An Arnoldian embrace of literature as "culture" bedeviled her throughout her career.

American books of any kind were particularly hard to come by (62); Buck comments wryly that "literature, it seemed, was English rather than American" (62). She mentions only Mark Twain as an American she read, though she failed to appreciate him (her mother found Twain also coarse, and didn't encourage her to read further). The family did, however, read a small number of American magazines: the *Delineator*, the *Century*, and two children's magazines, *St. Nicholas* and *The Youth's Companion* (63). Though the purpose was "to keep us in touch with the young of our own country" (63), these magazines reflected the America of an earlier time. Buck knew little of modern turmoil and the literary debate in magazines like the *Liberator* or *Munsey's* in the Progressive era, much as she would miss the later modernist debate in the *Nation*, the *New Republic*, or the *American Mercury*.

This isolation prompted a credulous embrace of America as a place of perfect equality, justice, order, and heroism. "America had always been the heavenly country," she proclaims, "the land where all was clean and kind and free" (*My Several Worlds* 275). Her mother taught her of heroes like Washington, Jefferson, and Madison (Conn 24) and constantly compared the dirt and poverty of China with the clean order and equality of America. Her Southern parents, who had departed America in the aftermath of the Civil War, taught her nothing of slavery or racial discrimination, nor of urban and rural poverty. The magazines they took added to this sense of unreality, for from them Buck "got the notion of incredible perfection in America, and I grew up misinformed and ripe for some disillusionment later" (*My Several Worlds* 63). Indeed, that initial millennial idealism and later disillusionment fueled her emerging political consciousness as a writer in the 1930s.

Both by education and in her daily life, however, Buck was more profoundly influenced by Chinese literary traditions. She studied every afternoon with a Confucian scholar, Mr. Kung, and learned the classical tradition thoroughly. That training helped her to become fluent in both written and spoken Chinese. He also taught her to look down on novel writing: "Novels, he taught me, cannot be considered literature. They are designed to amuse the idle and the illiterate, that is, those persons who cannot appreciate a true literary style and moral and philosophical content" (76). Mr. Kung was giving Buck the Chinese version of the "Great Books" debate, teaching a complicated literary tradition in language that excluded ordinary people's pleasures or experience.

But while she valued this classical education, Buck was also captivated by Chinese oral and written storytelling. She inhabited two worlds: "the small white clean Presbyterian American world of my parents and the big loving merry not-too-clean Chinese world" (10). There was, she explained, "no communication between them" (10). Her family was frequently the only white family in the town, and she grew up playing with Chinese children and listening to the talk of the women who worked in the house and were friends with her mother. As she wrote in a truncated biography of sorts for her 1933 short-story collection, *The First Wife,* she would beg her amah for stories every day, and hear of Buddhist miracles and Taoist magic (14–15). She grew up hearing ordinary people's stories about their lives.

This interest in storytelling led to her discovery of the Chinese popular tradition of novels. The cook told her stories from the three most famous Chinese novels: *The Three Kingdoms, All Men Are Brothers,* and *Dream of the Red Chamber* (*My Several Worlds* 57). These are sprawling, epic affairs; Buck would later translate *All Men Are Brothers* (more commonly known as *The Water Margin*), presenting it as a "great pageant of China" ("A Note by the Translator"). These Chinese novels became her most important literary models.

Part of this modeling connected, at least in Buck's literary imagination, with the Deweyan belief that art could provide vicarious experience. She advised American readers, "when you read this book forget it as a book. Think of it as a great procession of humanity" ("A Note by the Translator"). In that procession, readers should not attempt to "read every word or see everything," but in the end, "without [their] knowing it," will have indelible images of "certain unforgettable men and women, whose lives you have lived with them, across the seas and centuries" ("A Note by the Translator"). Buck may not have recognized her own connection with pragmatist aesthetics, but she advocates, by way of Chinese vernacular tradition, her own version of art as experience.

Buck's turn from classical to popular Chinese literature paralleled China's cultural and political transformations, which she was witnessing firsthand. China went through at three political upheavals from 1911 to 1927. Sudden "modernization" threw centuries-old traditions into doubt. Students championed science and technology and rejected the Confucian family system, which stressed deference to elders, arranged marriages, and female inferiority. These changes brought emotional turmoil to both traditional and modern Chinese. Buck interpreted this conflict with great sympathy in her short stories, collected in 1933 as *The First Wife;* these explore revolution through the innocent and often uncomprehending eyes of ordinary people.

At the same time, however, a literary renaissance was under way. "The aspect of the revolution which interested me most," Buck declares, "was still the literary one" (My Several Worlds 125). Young scholars were repudiating the formality of classical literature and advocating a new language—nationalist, political, and relevant to modern conditions. The grandfather of this literary movement was Lu Hsun. The son of a scholarly, monied family, Lu saw the complete breakup of that world owing to foreign imperialism (after the Boxer rebellion) and the Revolution of 1911. Appalled by the political excesses of his age, and by the fragile "democracy" that amounted to little more than a free hand for the strong over the weak, he retreated into scholarship until slightly before the 1911 May Fourth uprising.

Lu Hsun saw modern literature as the means to China's democratic transformation. Since "the most important task that lay ahead . . . was to change [the Chinese] in spirit," he explained, "I thought that literature might serve this purpose" (quoted in Kowallis 21). Lu and the young intellectuals who rallied behind him believed that the new literature would modernize and invigorate China. *New Youth,* first published in 1915, was the movement's intellectual center, advocating rejection of archaic Confucian language and an embrace the language of the common people. Chinese literary revolutionaries praised the same Chinese folk novels that Buck had loved as a child.

From these revolutionaries, Buck learned that literature could transform individuals and societies. By trusting and following the common people, a writer would discover the same nascent democratic spirit she found in Chinese folk culture. These two insights allied Buck with pragmatist aesthetics in America. (Chinese literary radicals, in fact, were influenced by John Dewey, who went on several lecture tours in China in the twenties.)

Her Nobel Prize acceptance speech (later published in pamphlet form by John Day) articulates Buck's Deweyan and Chinese-influenced beliefs about authorship. "In China," she explains, "art and the novel have always been widely separated" (*The Chinese Novel* 12). Art was the property of scholars, who were "kept . . . too busy with memorizing and copying the dead and classical past to see the present and its wrongs" (13). Formalistic, elitist, slaves to the past, scholars looked down on ordinary people and refused to acknowledge contemporary writing as valuable. "Happily for the Chinese novel" and "for the novelist," in fact, scholars considered novels unworthy of their attention. "The Chinese novel," Buck exulted, "grew as it like[d] out of its own soil, the common people, nurtured by that heartiest of sunshine, popular approval, and untouched by the cold and frosty winds of scholar's art" (17). Unconcerned with correct form, written in the vernacular so that the common people could understand, "the waters of the genius of story gushed out as they would, however the natural rocks allowed and the trees persuaded, and only common people came and drank and found rest and pleasure" (19).

A Chinese novelist, Buck claimed, wrote with

> his audiences always in mind and he found that the style which they loved best was one which flowed easily along, clearly and simply, in the short words which they themselves used every day, with no other technique than occasional bits of description, only enough to give vividness to a place or a person, and never enough to delay the story. Nothing must delay the story. Story was what they wanted. (24)

Drawing on her interpretation of the Chinese vernacular, Buck enshrines plot and accessible language as central to literature. Most essential, though, is to explore "human life as he finds it in himself or outside himself" (57). Thus, "a novelist must not think of pure literature as his goal. He must not even know this field too well, because people, who are his material, are not there" (59). "Pure literature," or an obsessive interest in form for its own sake, draws a writer away from the humanist values that make literature matter. Her Nobel Prize address demonstrates that what most critics identify as aesthetic defects were for Buck conscious choices, choices that resonate with pragmatist aesthetics.

Because of Buck's articulation of authorship, she found the assumptions behind American modernism inscrutable, particularly the formal experimentalism that seemed to disregard the common reader. With a much longer historical sense of the novel, she denied that any of these formal strategies were new. As she wrote in a humorous and pointed aside,

> I smile at the word experimental! Nothing is new, and everything has been done before. I read this week a reviewer's comment on a book,

> a criticism that the author had not used "the modern technique of cutback." New? Five hundred years ago Chinese novelists were using the cutback with consummate skill, and in Europe, whose history is comparatively recent, French writers were using the cutback when America was new. Joseph Conrad was a master of the cutback, and when I have used it, it has not occurred to me that I was doing anything modern, for I was not. (*My Several Worlds* 43)

Formal innovation was a means to reach, and please, readers. Buck seemed mystified that modern writing used technique to exclude, to appeal to only a small group of sophisticates.[1]

Buck didn't oppose "literary" to "popular"; she no more embraced anything popular than rejected everything literary. In fact, in 1939, this best-selling novelist attacked the "dictatorship of the best seller lists" much as antimiddlebrow critics had in the mid-twenties. She proclaims, "To read a book because others are reading it is no reason at all, and yet that is the only argument for consulting a best seller list. . . . We Americans who are so sensitive about freedom and independence in matters of government and laws controlling property submit our minds like ignorant lambs" ("Bestsellers" 4). This attempt to standardize reading hurts both individuals and the culture as a whole, because

> Reading, which is the basis of all true culture in a people, ought to spring out of individual interest. The humblest of persons has an interest and if he can read at all he will, if left to himself, search out books upon his interest, and from them his simple single interest will widen to include others. If it does not, at least he will have some pleasure out of his own mind and to that extent have genuine culture and will contribute to the culture of his fellows. (4)

Buck here appropriates modern critiques of materialism and standardization while subtly changing the terms of the debate. "Culture" wasn't an elite preserve but the individual's development of interest, which produces "pleasure out of his own mind." Culture is an egalitarian enterprise.

She further recuperates the popular (and her own writing career) by distinguishing between best-seller lists and occasional best sellers, which have "a life of their own." Best sellers are both born and made—that is, they sell both because of literary merit and because something in the "life" they depict "responds to a need of a moment, so that the two uniting create a vogue" (9). It is both literary and cultural virtuosity that make a book a best seller. Implicitly, however, Buck is asserting that a best seller contains both good writing and broad human significance. This was the John Day Company's claim for the success of *The Good Earth.* As Richard Walsh proclaimed in a radio broadcast in 1932, "THE GOOD EARTH, even though about Chinese people, is essentially and broadly a human book, and it therefore appealed to every type of reader" (Walsh Radio Broadcast November 1932).

The "broad human significance" of the true best seller was, for Buck, profoundly political. Though she didn't mention this in her Nobel Prize address, Buck knew that the Chinese vernacular tradition had fueled revolutions. Chinese monarchies had seen these popular novels as inherently subversive, and banned them over the centuries. Even "trashy" popular novels (or especially, "trashy" popular novels) were not simply idle entertainment. They were dangerous, powerful, transformative. Despite the message from the highbrow tradition, first from the Confucians, then from the American modernists, which made her sometimes doubt her status, Buck embraced the role of entertainer for the people with pride.

For her, value systems were not bankrupt; one could understand history and human behavior through simple cause and effect (*My Several Worlds* 52). "I have never been an evangelical missionary," she explains, erroneously, "and indeed abhor the general notion," but her "missionary beginnings" made her feel "responsible at least for what I can personally do about a given situation which needs mending" (371). After learning of the plight of Chinese slave girls as a teenager, she had determined that "wherever I saw evil and cruelty at work I would devote all I had to delivering its victims" (*My Several Worlds* 70), and after learning about injustice in America through an art exhibit about lynching, she used her influence to fight gender inequity, racism, and imperialism. In 1933, she attended a series of luncheons in Harlem hosted by Jessie Fauset. Langston Hughes christened her the modern "Harriet Beecher Stowe of the race" (Conn 259). Her critiques of imperialism in Asia provide a historical context for China that American diplomacy still cannot seem to grasp. As one of the most visible reformers of the 1930s, Buck spoke, as Canfield did sincerely and Fauset perhaps with more calculation, of her commitment to American democracy.

When Buck began her writing career, she understood very little about American literary markets. Having lived most of her life in China, she wrote about a people who had been represented in American letters mainly through caricature and sensationalism. She had no powerful friends in American publishing to advise her, no knowledge of how that marketplace functioned or how to master it. Her remarkable rise was a combination of hard work, opportunism, and luck.

Buck found her agent, David Lloyd, from an advertisement in an old magazine in the Shanghai bookshop (Conn 101); luckily for her, he was both honest and competent. He sent her first novel, *East Wind, West Wind,* to every publisher in New York. It was turned down by all of them, until he sent the manuscript to the new John Day and Company; when they accepted the novel for publication, it made the careers of both publisher Richard Walsh and Pearl Buck.

In Richard Walsh, Buck found the ideal gentleman-publisher—savvy, enthusiastic, supportive, and, as a new publisher in the Depression, eager for a best-selling writer. Walsh took a chance on Buck, despite what he perceived as a prejudice against novels about China, because he believed in her talent and thought she would develop into an important writer.

But Buck's most savvy move by far was marrying her publisher. Buck's relationship with Walsh was a remarkably successful literary partnership. Because her writings kept the publishing house afloat, Buck had tremendous leverage over the direction of John Day, leverage that allowed her to shape her own reputation and the character of the house itself, which single-handedly created a vogue for writing about Asia.

That leverage began, however, with the runaway success of *The Good Earth.*

"To draw aside the veil from one common man": *The Good Earth*

During a radio interview, in response to the question, "Do you feel that a book like THE GOOD EARTH brought its readers closer to the Chinese people?" Richard Walsh responded,

> I don't believe there can be the slightest doubt of that, for it shows the Chinese to be a people different only in custom, color and speech—yet living their life emotionally in much the same way as you and I. And speaking of that, I am sure that you would like to know that though I have never asked Mrs. Buck, I am sure that the

> tribute she values most is not the critical acclaim of her works—nor their great sales—but the realization that THE GOOD EARTH and its sequel SONS have helped to bring to the American people a deeper understanding of the Chinese people.[2]

In 1931, no book had ever approached the literary sensation of Pearl Buck's *The Good Earth.* Fortuitous circumstances helped to catapult the novel into fame. Dorothy Canfield, conscientiously reading the second-tier options for the BOMC selection committee, stumbled across the manuscript and was immediately caught up in the prose and the portrayal of life in Asia. Her enthusiasm inspired the rest of the committee to choose *The Good Earth* as its March selection in 1931.

The John Day Company was ecstatic, sending her a telegram announcing the selection and following it with a crowing letter:

> It is a glorious achievement for you and for THE GOOD EARTH. There has been little question in our minds that your novels are sure of an audience that will grow with every book published, but the tremendous impetus that this adoption gives to your popularity right at this moment promises a most gratifying short-cut to that audience. (Earl Newson to Buck 23 January 1931)

As the publishers explained, the BOMC would print 50,000 of its own copies to send to subscribers. Because "the effects of the adoption should not stop here, because the mere fact of the circulation of so large a number of copies of the book will be reflected in a larger sale of our edition through the book trade," John Day planned a higher first printing of 10,000 copies and was "already planning a large and extensive promotion and advertising campaign that we hope will stimulate the interest that The Book Club adoption will create" (Newson to Buck 23 January 1931). John Day was careful not to get Buck's hopes up about a best seller: "Just what the book will do in sales it is, of course, impossible to forecast, because, like all other books, it must pass that final judgment—the whim of American readers" (Newson to Buck 23 January 1931). They seemed confident, however, that they could master that whim; one can almost see Richard Walsh and his employees salivating.

They needn't have bothered trying to temper Buck's enthusiasm. She betrayed no knowledge about the Book-of-the-Month Club (Letter to

Richard Walsh 26 January 1931). Although Karen Leong suggests that she was playing the part of the literary ingenue, Buck's disavowal matches her later embrace of the Chinese anonymous artist, and is more credible since she actually was anonymous at the time: "The Chinese . . . take the artist as important only because of his art and are not interested in the personality of the artist and consider him unimportant except as a medium. But I understand from some of my friends that this is not the case with Americans" (Letter to Walsh January 1931).

It was indeed "not the case with Americans." The BOMC selection mattered a great deal; it changed Buck's life forever. *The Good Earth* was the best-selling novel of the first half of the 1930s; by June 1932, not a year and a half after its publication, it had sold nearly 180,000 copies. It was eventually made into a movie, with the highest advance paid, to that date, for the rights. Buck's triumphant Waldorf-Astoria dinner may have been her first indication of her newfound fame, but it all began with the BOMC selection and continued through Walsh's imaginative marketing campaign, which employed Buck's reticence and absence from the American scene as an asset.

Tensions between Buck's belief in *The Good Earth* as an act of service, to encourage understanding and sympathy between two vastly different cultures, and Walsh's commitment to efficient marketing and maximum sales, existed even before the novel's runaway success. In response to Walsh's suggestion of cuts to the manuscript, Buck wrote, "As to cutting, of course, my first impulse is against it. . . . But this is purely personal, and the book is not to belong to me, and I want it to be right for the ones who will read it" (Letter to Walsh 9 September 1930). To her agent David Lloyd she further elaborated on her intentions (and this message was forwarded to editors at John Day) when she explained that "these people in my book are very living for me, at least, and since they live for me, I hope they are alive for others, and that the Americans will see them primarily as people and not as Chinese, and so strange" (Letter toWalsh 25 June 1930). The John Day Company believed in *The Good Earth* as a notable work of art; it was also committed to encouraging sales through all means available. It not only advertised extensively, but also changed its advertising frequently to extend the remarkable run of the novel. Watching all of this from China, Buck wrote, "I am astounded at the immense amount of work all this advertising requires; I should think that any book would sell when propelled by such skillful methods!" (Letter to Walsh 30 July 1931).

Buck's missionary naiveté aside, John Day's advertising and marketing was certainly a large factor in the novel's success, for it connected it with American cultural trends that would make *The Good Earth* intelligible. When he first prepared the novel for publication, Walsh thought that to overcome the "prejudice here against books about China" (Letter to Buck 7 May 1931) he needed to market the book as a novel of the soil. By the third edition, however, this trend had passed, and he changed the cover of the book to a "Chinese motif," to take advantage of the "interest in China . . . whetted partly I think by the news and partly by the success of certain other books" (Letter to Buck 7 May 1931). The "Chinese motif," unsurprisingly, was a painting of a courtesan, which took advantage of American culture's fetish for the sexualized "Oriental" woman. Anticipating Buck's horrified response, Walsh offered this justification:

> I knew you did not want that. I did not want it myself. . . . But a best seller is somewhat in a position of a politician—"in the hands of its constituents." It seemed to us that restraint in the jacket, so long as it did not actually misrepresent the book, was less important then getting the inside of the book before the eyes of the largest possible number of readers. Therefore we turned to the best artist we knew of for the purpose . . . and he produced a design with the Chinese girl on it. . . . I do hope that it will not too much offend you. (Letter to Buck 7 May 1931)

Buck did, in fact, object to the cover "because it emphasized the wrong parts of the book, —I mean, drew attention from the life of the people and put it upon the incidents dealing with sex, which were only incidents, after all" (Letter to Walsh 3 June 1931).

Walsh further promoted *The Good Earth* by focusing on Buck as a "personality" in her own right. She was initially very anxious to avoid this role, not only because she respected the Chinese tradition of anonymity, but also for personal reasons; she had a retarded daughter whom she had recently placed in a full-time care facility in the United States, and she wanted that fact concealed. Walsh, however, insisted that she must participate in personal publicity. He wrote to her in July of 1931, when *The Good Earth* had sold 80,000 copies in four months, "I am very conscious of your wish to avoid the more distasteful forms of personal publicity and am trying to respect it just as far as possible in the face of the tremendous demand for personal information which is characteristic of the American public" (Letter to Buck 3 July 1931). *Publishers' Weekly,* in fact, contained a wry notice asking any acquaintances in China or America to come forward because "Pearl S. Buck, rather a reticent person herself, remains a trial to the publicity force of John Day." That very reticence, however, likely only increased the demand for Buck and her novel, for the public's curiosity was never sated.

Whatever liberties Walsh may have taken, and however pragmatically he used American prejudices and misconceptions to sell *The Good Earth,* it seems clear that he did so with the intention of getting people to read and then be moved by the novel. He wrote to Buck soon after publication: "I must not close this letter on the commercial note. I would rather say again how happy we are to have acted as the mechanism through which the beauty of your writing has reached so wide a public and through which you will have received some of the rewards of good work" (Letter to Buck 25 February 1931). Echoing Walsh, I don't want to leave the impression that *The Good Earth* is simply a product of exquisite marketing and good luck—although one should not underestimate the importance of either. As Buck's comments suggest, a popular novel must satisfy some larger cultural desire. For reviewers, *The Good Earth* created vicarious experience of an unknown culture. In other words, it provided a quintessential middlebrow reading experience.

Many of the gushing reviews indicate how *The Good Earth* inspired sympathetic understanding. Buck portrayed a China that had never been seen in America, without cherry blossoms, opium, or courtesans. As the reviewer for the *New Statesman* explained, "Here no flutes of jade sound delicately across the moonlit courts, no meditative general sets brush to paper to catch for ever the susurration of dead leaves outside his door, no intricacy of self-abasing compliment unwinds itself from the lips of beggar or mandarin" ([Review of *The Good Earth*] 430). As a result, "the ordinary, flesh-and-blood, everyday Chinaman" emerges from the "screens and veils and mirrors of artistic and poetic convention which nearly always make him, to the Western reader's eye, a flat and unsubstantial figure of a pale-coloured ballet" (430). Though the text's "authenticity" was performed, it appeared to strip away exotic stereotypes in favor of a true image of China. What critics noticed was the overwhelming humanity of Wang Lung. Nancy Evans's review for *The Bookman* shows the impression the novel gave of immediate, mystical communion:

> If the purpose of the novel is to affect the emotions by revealing human life, then *The Good Earth* may be called great. To read this story of Wang Lung, Chinese farmer, is to be slowly and deeply purified; and when the last page is finished it is as if some significant part of one's own days were over. Though I may never see a rice-field, I shall always feel that I have lived for a long time in China. The strange power of a western woman to make an alien civilization seem as casual, as close, as the happenings of the morning is surprising; but it is less amazing than her power to illuminate the destiny of man as it is in all countries and at all times by quietly telling the story of one poor Wang Lung. It is true that religion, clothing, tradition, food and even the skies themselves are different from the things we know; and yet these differences are of no consequence. (324)

Evans's reading gives evidence of the kind of vicarious experience, of deep sympathy and secular conversion (for she is "slowly and deeply purified"), that middlebrow authors seek to create. Buck both preserves difference—Evans recognizes that the "alien civilization" differs in every particular—and makes that difference "of no consequence."

Part of the sense of mystical kinship comes from the style of the novel. There is a sort of prophetic simplicity to this epic of a common man's life. John Day Company explained in an advertisement that *The Good Earth*'s "singular beauty" came from the "author's uncommon lingual experience." Buck composed her novels in Chinese and then translated them into English (Lloyd Letter to Mr. Rimington 25 June 1930). This produced a style that many readers could only recognize as scriptural; it carried authority and the aura of authenticity. As the advertisement concluded, "Because these people were never alien to her, because she has shared their lives and their speech, she has been able 'to draw aside the veil' from the life of one common man and his family."

"To draw aside the veil" (the advertisement cleverly reminds the reader of the Proustian epigraph), Buck must show that cultural differences between China and America don't alter the shared humanity underneath. She wrote to her agent David Lloyd that the success of her novel proves that Americans "would like the Chinese if they saw them for the human beings that they are, differing only in non-essentials from the Americans themselves and all other humankind" (quoted in David Lloyd to Richard Walsh 28 April 1931).

To show that cultural differences are "non-essential," Buck uses an ordinary peasant. To her the Chinese peasant was the model for goodness and integrity, because these farmers "were the most real, the closest to the earth, to birth and death, to laughter and to weeping" (*My Several Worlds* 146). She looked for "reality" among them, "and among them I found the human being as he most nearly is" (146). Chinese peasants can be seen to share with Jefferson's farmer citizen the agrarian myth.

And who is this Wang Lung, "the human being as he most nearly is"? He is, first and foremost, a sensual creature. His joy in marriage is not only the ease of having someone else serve him, but simple lust. In "exultation" on his wedding night, he simply "seized her" (*The Good Earth* 18). Later, when he becomes enamored of a prostitute, his desire becomes more stylized; her smallness and helplessness, "her pointed little feet and her curling helpless hands" (144), keep him "fevered and thirsty" (131). Despite his wife O-lan's devotion and loyalty, he cannot love her because she is not beautiful. And even as an old man, he still feels desire, and takes a young girl as a concubine. Sex is a basic impulse for Wang Lung, and he satisfies it frankly. The novel's emphasis on sex alienated many "pious Christians" (in Peter Conn's phrase) who considered *The Good Earth* "coarse," and Buck embraced that label, insisting that Americans needed to get over their prudishness (Conn 128).

And yet, Wang Lung is not simply an animal; he is also industrious and tender-hearted. This is crucial to establishing China's humanity, for the American stereotype of China emphasizes polygamy and slavery as proof of its misogyny and savagery. Wang Lung, though raised in a culture that ostensibly places women last, is too kind to treat women badly. When he marries O-lan, he "desired suddenly that she should like him as her husband and then he was ashamed" (*The Good Earth* 19), because in his culture he should only care that "she fulfilled her duty" (21). Buck carefully juxtaposes the cultural (a wife is to serve) with the universal (marriage and sex are more than simple obligation). Wang Lung cares about O-lan, but his cultural inheritance inhibits his innate goodness: "He was ashamed of his own curiosity and of his interest in her. She was, after all, only a woman" (21). Guilt over infidelity is also a universal human emotion—as universal as adultery. When O-lan reproaches him for sleeping with Lotus, Wang Lung feels ashamed, and then, "he was rough because he was ashamed and would not acknowledge his shame in his heart" (134). Though his shame doesn't change his behavior, his acknowledgment of O-lan's feelings and his own guilt make his taking of a second wife cruel *and* understandable. The evil Fu Manchu becomes the indulgent, kind, and very human Wang Lung, who gives way to rages but also lovingly protects his simple-minded daughter; who beats his son from jealousy but for whom family obligations are paramount; who remains, in poverty or wealth, what he always was, a man who acts from impulse and instinct. Even when Wang Lung behaves in morally reprehensible ways, his feelings and reactions are perfectly comprehensible as "universal" human responses. His sensuality and his selfishness are counteracted by a goodness that reassured American readers about their own mores.

Buck further assures readers of the universality of human experience with a Chinese example of the American dream. As she explains in a letter, one Chinese characteristic is "the fundamental democracy that has always been here—men rising out of the common mass, who are yet earthy and common themselves. . . . A poor man has always a chance at rough justice—if he watches his chance. Masses of common people can rise—do rise—and put down a government in their own crude way" (Letter to Walsh 25 June 1930). *The Good Earth* was perfectly oriented toward an American culture that was committed to the idea of personal effort and upward mobility but was shifting left, in the thirties, toward more collective support for the poor and for economic justice. The novel both embraces the importance of class and disavows it, a conflict familiar to middle-class readers who were in 1931 just coming to terms with the Depression.

Though Wang Lung is poor, he never thinks of himself so until famine forces him to work in the city. He then "lived in the rich city as alien as a rat in a rich man's house that is fed on scraps thrown away, and hides here and there and is never a part of the real life of the house" (75). The very richness of the city, he learns, is based on "the foundation of poverty" (80). The city poor have faces permanently set in scowls from "straining at loads too heavy for them" (81), and street preaching and growing dissatisfaction feed an emerging class consciousness. A passerby teaches Wang Lung that suffering cannot continue forever, for "when the rich are too rich there are ways, and when the poor are too poor there are ways" (84). Student organizers preach communism on street corners.

Wang Lung's economic rise, in fact, is enabled by a kind of class revolution. The poor of the city riot and loot the homes of the rich, and O-lan, familiar with the hiding places of the owners, discovers jewels that allow

Wang Lung to purchase land and become a landlord. Wang Lung himself steals from a rich man to pay for their journey home—a rich man described in loathsome detail:

> He was a great fat fellow, neither old nor young. . . . The great yellow rolls of his flesh doubled over his breasts and over his belly and in the mountains of his cheeks his eyes were small and sunken as a pig's eyes. When he saw Wang Lung he shook all over and yelled out as though his flesh had been stuck with a knife. (98)

The rich man's decadence makes Wang Lung's theft a virtuous act. Implicit in the narrative is a spontaneous land and wealth redistribution that differs from Chinese Communism only in scale.

Buck, however, steps back from the ideological implications of this story; or perhaps more accurately, she emphasizes individualism to sidestep the class issues implicit in Wang Lung's rise. A simple man from the land, he cannot understand how the rich exploit the poor; to him poverty comes from concrete natural disasters, like famine: "When there was rain and sun in proportion so that the seed would sprout in the land and the stalk bear grain, he did not consider himself poor" (89). He is never able to generalize from his own experiences. He knows only that he didn't belong "to this scum which clung to the walls of a rich man's house" (87), but to the land; and when through theft and labor he becomes a rich man himself, he benefits from other men's labor and behaves as badly as any landlord before him. He hates the poor who live in the courts of the great house he buys in town: "he said to himself that they were filthy and he picked his way among them with his nose up and breathing lightly because of the stink they made" (212). Buck suggests this pattern when she describes the evicted poor "muttering that one day they would come back even as the poor do come back when the rich are too rich" (224). But these are only hints; the novel as a whole disavows class consciousness; Wang Lung, a farmer, exists beyond designations of rich and poor.

Indeed, Wang Lung is protected from communism because of his connection with the land. It is *The Good Earth's* insistence on the innate virtue of tilling that makes it a "novel of the soil" and connects it with the American agrarian theme. Although America is no longer (to the degree that it was) a nation of farmers, the power of that myth, and its connection with town meetings and ideal democracy, remains strong. Richard

Walsh drew on these assumptions to help guide *The Good Earth* into the mainstream. He suggested that Buck write an article about China for an agricultural magazine, for "with the life of China being agricultural, I feel that to reach the vast number of American farmers with such an article as you would write, would contribute greatly to that understanding," especially since "the steady progress of THE GOOD EARTH . . . is now carrying it out into the small towns and rural territory" (Letter to Buck 6 August 1951). The novel's commitment to the land as the ultimate virtue resonated with Americans nostalgic for the era of farming, and further established the novel's "universality."

Even for many moderns, who had rejected all previous dogma and religion, there remained a nostalgia and reverence for the land, for a life that, they felt, had been irrevocably lost in the industrial age.[3] Wang Lung's purest and most satisfying connection with his land comes in the early days of his marriage to O-lan. When she works in the fields with him, he feels the joy of communion:

> There was only this perfect sympathy of movement of turning this earth of theirs over and over to the sun, this earth which formed their home and fed their bodies and made their gods. . . . Some time, in some age, bodies of men and women had been buried there, houses had stood there, had fallen, and gone back into the earth, their bodies also. Each had his turn at this earth. They worked on, moving together—together—producing the fruit of this earth—speechless in their movement together. (*The Good Earth* 22)

Working with O-lan in the fields provides Wang Lung with the closest thing to religious abstraction this sensual man will ever encounter. O-lan is an earth mother who reveals the properties of the land herself. She is transfigured: "Her face was wet and streaked with the earth. She was as brown as the very soil itself" (22). And after their child's birth, O-lan is also fecund, Madonnalike:

> The child lay on an old torn quilt on the ground, asleep. When it cried the woman stopped and uncovered her bosom to the child's mouth, sitting flat upon the ground, and the sun beat down upon them both. . . . The woman and the child were as brown as the soil and they sat there like figures made of earth. There was the dust

> of fields upon the woman's hair and upon the child's soft black head. (29)

The moments of deepest significance—contentment, friendship, children—are all bound up with the land itself.

So intimate is Wang Lung's connection with the earth that his religion comes directly from the soil. On their land, his grandfather has built a temple in which "sat two small, solemn figures, earthen, for they were formed from the earth of the fields about the temple" (15). The very gods are made of earth and, when neglected, return to the earth, just as all people will eventually return to the earth. Through his connection with the soil, Wang Lung learns humility. His religious outbursts come when he fears that he is too fortunate, and immediately gives devotions to the land. After the birth of his first son,

> He thought of this at first with joy and then with a pang of fear. It did not do in this life to be too fortunate. The air and the earth were filled with malignant spirits who could not endure the happiness of mortals, especially of such as are poor. He turned abruptly into the candlemaker's shop, who sold incense also, and there he bought four sticks of incense, one for each person in his house, and with these four sticks he went into the small temple of the gods of the earth, and he thrust them into the cold ashes of the incense he had placed there before, he and his wife together. He watched the four sticks well lit and then went homeward, comforted. These two small, protective figures, sitting staidly under their small roof—what a power they had! (28–29)

When the land grows unfruitful, he curses the gods, and after the famine he sees that "they were piteous to behold, their features washed from their faces" (103). Even when he curses them for not helping him, he "unwillingly" decides to give them incense because, "after all, they have power over earth" (103). It is only when Wang Lung, through riches, is separated from the daily tilling that he grows forgetful of the earth gods.

Wang Lung's devotion to the earth, no matter what his failings as a husband or a father, is absolute. Even when facing starvation, he refuses to sell, shrieking at the profiteers who have approached him, "I will never sell the land! . . . Bit by bit I will dig up the fields and feed the earth itself to the children and when they die I will bury them in the land, and I and my wife and my old father, even he, we will die on the land that has given us birth!" (61). And even when he is suffering as a poor man in the city, "the memory of his land . . . lying back there, far away, it is true, but waiting and his own, filled him with peace" (74).

When Wang Lung is close to the soil, he is at his most virtuous, and when he is separated from it, he is led into problems, if not "sin." It is clear, for example, that he would never have gone to teahouses if he had not been idle because of his wealth and the floods. His father is horrified by the presence of a "harlot" in his house, proclaiming, "I had one woman and my father had one woman and we farmed the land" (150). When Wang Lung is cured of his "sickness" of lust, it is through the land; when he returns to labor, Buck explains, he overcomes this obsession.

The cities are dangerous because people there are so separated from the land. When his children steal in order to supplement their diet, Wang Lung "is angry and afraid in his heart because his sons were growing into thieves here in this city" (80). Only when influences alien to a life of the soil (like city thieving and teahouse concubines) enter does Wang Lung beat his children, and in the city, after beating his second son, he proclaims, "We must get back to the land" (80). It is the source of all virtue, and separation from it, whether through poverty or riches, defeats virtue.

In this world, Christianity's metaphors are too abstract to relate to the life of a farmer, as the earth gods do. One day, a terrifying foreigner with "eyes as blue as ice," "a hairy face," and "a great nose projecting beyond his cheeks like a prow beyond the sides of a ship" (88) hands Wang Lung a paper that he is too frightened to refuse. He sees "the picture of a man, white-skinned, who hung upon a cross-piece of wood" (88). With "horror and increasing interest," he takes the paper home and discusses "its possible" meaning with his father and sons. His father is sure that "surely this was a very evil man to be thus hung," and Wang Lung takes the picture as a threat. Christianity is inscrutable here. O-lan is undisturbed, and "sewed [the paper] into a shoe sole together with other bits of paper she picked up here and there to make the soles firm" (89). This suggests why the novel at first deeply offended Christian missionaries: Christianity, in this world, is just so much paper.

Tending the land and making crops grow means more than racial identity in belonging to a country. The end of *The Good Earth* seems to identify a root cause of the modern world's displacement in a rejection of the soil. When Wang Lung overhears his sons planning to sell the land, he is adamant: "if you sell the land, it is the end" (260). Buckthus identifies a solution to the West's modern crisis, finding it in one of the cultures most alien to Western consciousness.

Despite Buck's focus on universality, she also exploits the exotic in her novel. If this is an epic of the soil, it is also a local-color story. The author developed her literary tastes from reading *The Atlantic Monthly,* the original source of such writing, and her first published piece in America, in the *Atlantic,* was a sketch of China that would not have been out of place thirty or forty years earlier. A bemused contrast of American moderns and a relatively unchanged culture, "In China, Too" represents a tranquil, graceful, ordered world in blessed contrast to the social turmoil of the United States. As she writes near the beginning of the article, "Dancing on six inches or so of floorspace, the discussion of knees and necks and petting parties, the menace of the movies and the divorce question, are a far cry from this tranquil corner of my cool, wide veranda" (*My Several Worlds* 163). Though there are changes under way in the traditional society, as represented by a girl who unbinds her feet, the dominant tone is permanence. The modern Chinese girl is horrified at the thought of men and women walking and talking together; her reserve shows how impotent such attempts at change are. Buck provides the reader with images that meet orientalist tastes. The queenly opium addict is one such stereotype; she sees on the street "a ponderous dowager, in plum-colored satin, with proud drooping eyelids, opium-stained teeth, and a long bamboo pipe, silver-tipped, which she uses as a cane" (*My Several Worlds* 163). Buck here invokes the memory of the Empress Dowager, the Emperor's courtesan who ruled China for forty years in the nineteenth century and was seen in the West as the brutal instigator of the Boxer Rebellion (and about whom she would later write a novel, *Imperial Woman*). Since the reader has no idea what each of Buck's details—"plum-colored satin," "drooping eyelids" which are also "proud," "opium-stained teeth," a "silver-tipped" pipe—signifies culturally (rank? widowhood? eccentricity?), they combine in an impression of otherness, inscrutable and fascinating.

This tendency toward exotic surface detail carries over to *The Good Earth,* as seen in the wedding preparations for the bride of Wang Lung's oldest son:

> Then they dressed her in garments she had brought from her home; white flowered silk next to her sweet virgin flesh and then a light coat of sheep's wool of the finest and most curling kind, and then the red satin garments of marriage. And they rubbed lime upon her forehead high and smooth and square for her new estate. Then they painted her with powder and with red paint, and with a brush they drew out in two long slender lines her eyebrows, and they set upon her head the bride's crown and the beaded veil, and upon her small feet they put shoes, embroidered, and they painted her fingertips and scented the palms of her hands, and thus they prepared her for marriage. (190)

Buck doesn't explain why a curling coat of sheep's wool and red satin garments are appropriate, nor does she explain the excessive painting and primping, which long signified prostitution and promiscuity to Americans.

In fact, so many of Buck's images of Chinese life seemed to satisfy American expectation of the exotic that many Asians studying in America objected. Younghill Kang, who had published a narrative of his childhood in Korea, wrote a scathing review of the novel. He detected Christian moralizing: "Mrs. Buck, the daughter of a missionary, refuses from the start of her book to admit that any relation between individuals involving neither love and good times nor souls' consolation is not and never could have been marriage" (185). None of the central events could ever have taken place, including the rape of slaves. "To a Western reader," such a book may be "very moving" (185), but based as it is on romantic love, the entire picture is false.

Kang's objections to *The Good Earth* indicate his upper-class intellectual background and his lack of familiarity with customs in Northern China, a point Buck was careful to make in her rebuttal of this review. His suggestion that Buck's images could easily replace one set of stereotypes with another is well taken, however. It is likely that many American readers left *The Good Earth* impressed more by China's strangeness than by any kinship with their own country.

But even this may work in *The Good Earth*'s favor. If Buck, after so strongly emphasizing Wang Lung's common humanity, could still leave readers with a respect for the difference—the otherness—of Chinese culture, then she may have walked the tightrope between sameness and difference better than did most middlebrow writers. For her part, she was most satisfied by the Chinese reviews, which were nearly all positive. These, she claimed,

> go to prove what I have always felt true, that the Chinese are wise enough in all common sense to appreciate the truth about themselves, for they know what human nature is, having had the deepest experience of any race now in the world. They ask only that the approach to that truth be human and sympathetic, and not critical in an abusive or prejudiced way. Nor do they like any more the sentimental approach. Indeed they do ask no more than to be held what they truly are, an essential part of the human family. (Letter to John Day 22 July 1931)

If Buck's ultimate aim was to make American readers sympathetic to the Chinese people and culture, then *The Good Earth* succeeded, for China became an interest and a focus in American culture in the thirties in an unprecedented way.

From "the Orient" to Asia: Multicultural Middlebrow

Pearl Buck took seriously her stated goal of explaining the East to the West, and her efforts went beyond her own widely read and highly publicized novels of China (which included two sequels to *The Good Earth,* two biographies of her missionary parents, and several other novels in the thirties). She used her fame to introduce more radical political viewpoints of, and many writers from, China.

Perhaps the most significant effort she made for Chinese culture in America was her mammoth translation of the thirteenth-century Chinese novel *Shui Hu Chuan.* Buck spent more than five years translating this enormous sprawling work, which, in the English version, contained over 1,200 pages of episodic adventure, warfare, and drinking. It details the development of a group of "righteous robbers" who band together in a mountain stronghold. It is most similar to the picaresque novel in the European tradition, but longer and broader in scope, providing an unparalleled image of Chinese culture that, in its overwhelming variety, shatters any simple stereotypes of the "Orient." It also challenges common Western assumptions about the history of the novel by displaying a much older tradition on the other side of the world. Buck insisted that the novel be kept "unabridged, because it *is* a classic" (Letter toWalsh 3 May 1932). Richard Walsh, anxious, I think, to please his best-selling author, was committed to publishing and promoting the novel at a loss. He titled it, in an appropriately middlebrow strategy, *All Men Are Brothers,* because "It has the quality I have been reaching for, a largeness, suggesting an epic, and it seems to me justified (even though the robbers killed a good many thousands of men) by the spirit of the book and the fact that it is accepted as Communist literature" (Letter to Buck 27 February 1933). He lobbied for a Book-of-the-Month Club selection so that the novel would be both inexpensive and well-known. Henry Seidel Canby, however, eventually decided that the novel didn't have enough mainstream appeal for a primary selection, although it was favorable mentioned in the *Book-of-the-Month Club News;* it was published in a two-volume set and a much more expensive, smaller run. Its sales were modest, and Buck and the John Day Company shared the loss. But the cultural influence of *All Men Are Brothers* extended far beyond its sales. John Day promoted it as a "book that has to be read because it ranks with the great folk tales and epics of all nations and all time—we have had the classics of this type from many other languages—now for the first time we have the great Chinese epic of folklore" (Advertisement 27 February 1933). Walsh's points of comparison were varied and far-reaching: *Robin Hood, the Arabian Nights, Don Quixote, the Iliad, the Odyssey, Gulliver's Travels, the Canterbury Tales, King Arthur, Paul Bunyan, Les Miserables, Marco Polo.* Americans became aware of the Chinese literary tradition, and the novel, under its distinctive title, entered the popular lexicon in the thirties. The two most famous Western journalists covering communist China in the thirties, Edgar Snow and Agnes Smedley, referred to *All Men Are Brothers* without any explanation, which indicates that they could assume a familiarity that no longer exists today.

Many modern presses and writers (Alfred A. Knopf epitomizes this trend) tried to influence American culture through the translation of European highbrow literature. Pearl Buck here attempted something different, introducing Chinese folk culture to American literary circles. The Chinese writer Lin Yutang, in an adulatory review, articulated the cultural challenge of Buck's translation. "Will this [translation]," he concluded his piece, "be her most successful attempt to make the Americans uncomfortable and to a certain extent change their fashion of reading?" (np). *All Men Are Brothers* may not have changed American reading patterns, but it certainly challenged Eurocentric assumptions about the novel, form, and culture, and opened serious discourse on China.

But Buck's drive to enlarge Asia's visibility in American culture didn't end with this translation. After the success of *The Good Earth,* the John Day Company had become thoroughly identified with Asian subjects. Married to Richard Walsh and serving as an editor in her own right, Buck helped John Day introduce many Asian writers to the American public. Perhaps the most successful was Lin Yutang, a Chinese intellectual whose novel *A Moment in Peking* was a Book-of-the-Month Club selection in 1939. Buck and Walsh also took over the journal *Asia* and transformed it from a tourist magazine into an influential policy journal that published the leading voices on Asia of its day. *Asia* encouraged a range of political perspectives, including those of explicitly communist writers. It published articles by Lin Yutang, Bertrand Russell, Charles Beard, Agnes Smedley, Helen Foster Snow, Margaret Mead, Anna Louise Strong, and Rabindranath Tagore, the 1913 Nobel Prize winner from India.

Buck, then, used her fame to promote American understanding of Asia. In her difficult role of serving as a mediator for China, she attempted to replace American "Oriental" stereotypes with more authentic depictions, even as she respected the many significant differences within Chinese culture. Authenticity remained an obsession for many critics, dating from the publication of *The Good Earth.* Eda Walton's review notes "a flatness of emotional tone" in her book "which is not characteristic of Knut Hamsun's studies of the toiler in the earth, nor again of the autobiographical narrative of a Korean childhood and boyhood, 'The Grass Roof.'" These writers' superiority comes "from their own traditional knowledge and racial inheritance"; Buck being an "Occidental writer," is less convincing and exciting. Walton concludes that "'The Good Earth' lacks the imaginative intensity, the lyrical quality, which someone who had actually farmed Chinese soil might have been able to give it" (94). There is no question that Buck's perspective was not Chinese, but rather an amalgam of American ideology and the diverse China she had encountered. For this very reason, however, she could better explain China to American readers. Someone who had actually farmed Chinese soil would not necessarily have been able to produce a narrative that appeared authentic to American reviewers.

Buck used her fame and her audience to inveigh against racism, sexism, and imperialism. So outspoken were her attacks on the hypocrisy of American racism and the outrage of British imperialism in China that Dorothy Canfield gently chastised her for not considering her audience's desire to feel hopeful and virtuous (Letter to Buck 27 August 1943). Buck's secular missionary zeal made Canfield's measured risks seem cowardly in the thirties. Kang Liao gives Buck credit for transforming American attitudes toward China, leading to the 1943 repeal of the Chinese exclusion act and to American support against Japanese invasion in the late thirties. As Liao puts it, "[Americans] thought the Japanese were invading the homeland of Wang Lung and O-lan, killing their children. . . . The Chinese were no longer just an abstract concept for them but had taken concrete shapes in their minds as the characters created by Pearl Buck" (81). Though such larger cultural shifts are difficult to trace, it seems plausible to say that Pearl Buck's influence played a large part in whatever transformation did occur. Karen Leong marks Buck as a key interpreter of what she calls "the China mystique," a version of China that was more positive than stereotypes that preceded it. Through Buck's multicultural middlebrow authorship, China, while still exotic, became surprisingly familiar to American middle-class readers.

FOUR

Proletarian Middlebrow

Josephine Herbst, Radicalism, and Bourgeois Redemption

In the 1960s, in response to a query from a professor, Josephine Herbst articulated her vision of reading and writing communities in terms that would have shocked literary critics of the thirties, who had found her writing dispassionate:

> If you are teaching work of the thirties I believe it would be important to engage the students and a group and to teach the literature of the period as an involvement with life. For the thirties, and the purposes of literature, the involvement was too heavy to make perfect literature, but it broke ground for exciting vistas. Often too documentary, sometimes too much reportage, it still had a vital connection with more than events. But the events were also crucial and the major core of our ill-adjustments remains. . . . The thirties has more often been maligned than not; it happens to have been a lively period in spite of the depression, lively in the arts and lively in human mingling. People cared. It was a decade when people believed in the possibility of their own powers. Farmers did fight for what they believed to be their rights; workers did believe that they could have the right to unionize. . . . But literature is centered always in the values of the human, and for that reason it can shed light far

> beyond any document, any statistic. . . . Without memory, without some connectedness, there is nothing. Hence, I suppose, some of the tendency to exalt "meaninglessness." Every major novelist from way back has understood that there is always, somewhere, some time, a sense of the meaninglessness of it all, but there must also be a meaning to so-called meaninglessness or no writing would accrue. To make clarity out of obscurity, to clear a path in the jungle—that's the thing—and a good reader is as important in the long run as a good writer. They need each other. (Letter to William A. Sutton 6 February 1968)

Herbst's passionate engagement with social issues isn't surprising in a writer best known for her proletarian trilogy—*Pity Is Not Enough, The Executioner Waits,* and *Rope of Gold.* Herbst had always been known as the most modern and rebellious of writers, one who worked for H .L. Mencken, drank with Ernest Hemingway, gossiped with Katherine Anne Porter, and marched with Michael Gold. Her first two novels were devastating indictments of middle-class life, embodying the "terrible honesty" Ann Douglas defines as the epitome of American modernism. Her embrace of proletarian literature in the 1930s placed her in the vanguard of literary rebels once again, "going left" with a host of others.

What *is* surprising is her insistence that "literature is centered always in the values of the human," her focus on the continuity of art and life, and her belief in the symbiotic relationship between reader and writer. She defines a writing aesthetic remarkably consistent with Dewey's notion of pragmatist aesthetics, one consistent with Dorothy Canfield, Pearl Buck, even Jessie Fauset. Herbst, as we shall see, would have violently disavowed any connection with such popular women's writers.

This connection between literary proletarianism and middlebrow authorship has been unexplored. Josephine Herbst represents this counterintuitive connection between two modes of writing focused on political conversion and affect, particularly through women's writing and middle-class family dramas. Herbst, I want to argue, was a closet middlebrow author, who came closest to coming out during the 1930s.

Modern Rebellion and the "Gents": Herbst's Construction of Authorship

Unlike the other writers in this study, Herbst came to authorship through the cultural rebellion of the moderns, and despite significant differences, she retained this primary identification. For Herbst, writing began as a rebellion against the rigid conformity of Sioux City, Iowa. Writing would save her from the mindless toil and suffocating conventionality of middle-class small-town life, a trap she and her sister Helen had to escape at any cost. As she wrote years later in a draft of her memoir, "It was in Iowa that I was an exile; not in Europe" (quoted in Ehrhardt 146). She embraced sexual liberation; while working in New York in the early twenties, she had an affair with the married playwright Maxwell Anderson, and then, at his insistence, had an abortion. Her common-law marriage with John Herrman, whom she met in Paris, became respectable only when his parents bullied them into a legal ceremony.

Herbst lived in Berkeley, Seattle, New York, Berlin, and Paris; after she met Herrman in Europe, New York became her home base. In Greenwich Village, she knew many famous and soon-to-be-famous writers, including H. L. Mencken, Katherine Anne Porter, Ernest Hemingway, Malcolm Cowley, Michael Gold, James Farrell, John Dos Passos, Claude McKay, Caroline Gordon, Allen Tate, Robert Penn Warren, Kenneth Burke, and Hart Crane.[1] These unpublished writers, who would later be canonized as modernists, Harlem Renaissance writers, or Southern Agrarians, were accumulating cultural capital in opposition to the marketplace (even though many would become financially successful). Herbst was living the myth of the modern writer, a life she had moved to New York to find. As Elinor Langer describes the atmosphere, "The streets of the Village are thick with writers. . . . In those days a volume of Joyce or Stein carried under the arm was sufficient, like a political button, to establish membership in the modern movement" (88). It was the writer's life that mattered—living in garrets, drinking in speakeasies, looking down on the philistine publishers and the sell-outs who made fortunes; "writers are the audience that matters" (92), not middle-class readers.

Her first two published novels, *Nothing Is Sacred* and *Money for Love* (published in 1928 and 1929, respectively), are biting satires on the failures of the middle class; they expose the thin veneer of respectability overlaying its moral bankruptcy, and inability to really love or live with honor. Herbst's novels offended not just the larger literary culture but her own family. Criticized for fictionalizing her brother-in-law's embezzlement, "Josie wrote her father that she 'had to write that or never write again,' and throughout her life, confronted by hostile people who found themselves in her stories, her justification was much the same" (100). Herbst's definition of authorship as the telling of a harmful or painful truth is opposed to that of Canfield, who consistently chose people over fiction.

Herbst seems a textbook modernist—writing as a lifestyle; writing primarily for other writers; unconcerned with readers' emotional identification and experience; seeing cultural rebellion as a primary responsibility of authorship. She identified with precisely the mode of authorship, in other words, that would supplant and devalue middlebrow authorship.

Yet that identification didn't satisfy her financial or emotional needs; it didn't quite fit. After moving to New York after World War I and struggling in a series of underpaid office jobs, she worked for H. L. Mencken, reading manuscripts for pulp magazines as well as the *American Mercury.* She described the job to her sister Helen:

> I like the new job—it's amusing. You ought to see the stories I get—some are imbecilical—so stupid—so silly. I just read them all day long & talk & gossip & eat & smoke. It's huge fun. I'm on the editorial staff & the job really has possibilities. Of course all the magazines are flippant & "smarty" & superficial & cynical but it's good experience & will get me somewhere better afterwards. So far I've had only bluff & it's time I had something else to back me. Mr. Mencken is first rate if his magazines aren't. Hardly a publisher in NY accepts a book without Mencken first approving it. He *is* a real critic. (quoted in Langer 63)

Herbst looks down on Mencken's magazine empire; "flippant & 'smarty' & superficial & cynical," Mencken, she has discovered quickly, is as implicated in capitalist pandering to the middle class as any despised genteel institution. When she hits the "big time," she discovers that selling literature is not unlike selling farm equipment, which is what her father did—and that the king of modern rebellion, H. L. Mencken, is a businessman who sells trash to the same public he vilifies in the *Smart Set.* Her discontent came out in her political protests—for striking dockworkers in Seattle, against the Sacco and Vanzetti executions—and led to her increased involvement in social protest in the 1930s. Herbst's attempt to distance Mencken the critic from Mencken the businessman preserved her image of the modern writer and served her own interest; she tried to use this connection when seeking a publisher for her first novel.

Herbst's status as a woman writer and her focus on gender issues made her identification with modern authorship even more complicated. She was not accepted as a "full" member of the club because she was a woman. Katherine Anne Porter and Herbst both believed they were excluded from publications and prestige because of their gender (Langer 91). Most of the women in their circle were wives, not writers (89). Herbst and Porter felt at a disadvantage with the "Gents," as they called them. Malcolm Cowley called them the "talkingest women I ever met," but even that designation, in a group of champion talkers, shows how unusual women like this were (89). (Dorothy Parker is, I believe, the exception that proves the rule.)

This sense of exclusion was particularly important for Herbst. Her writing was deeply concerned with women's issues. Her focus on abortion, on sexuality and career, on mothers and daughters, all mark her as a kind of renegade "women's novelist." Herbst had two traumatic experiences with abortion—her own, which she obtained under pressure from her married lover Maxwell Anderson, and hardly spoke of to anyone, including her own family; and shortly thereafter, her sister's, which resulted in infection and death. Julia Ehrhardt argues that these two experiences haunted Herbst her entire writing career, dominating her artistic vision and her romantic relationships (143).

Despite this primary concern with women's issues, however, Herbst shied away from women's magazines and other forums that focused on middle-class women. It may seem strange to suggest that Herbst felt isolated. A large number of women writers were living and thriving in and around New York—Kathleen Norris, Fanny Hurst, Edna Ferber, and later Pearl Buck. But these middlebrow authors were writing in very different forums, for a very different audience. They might have lived on another planet, so far were they from the folkways of Greenwich Village. They were treated only with disdain by the "Smart Set," who made them the image of consumerism and mediocrity.

Herbst participated in the lampooning of women's middlebrow audiences. She regularly assailed the institutions of genteel culture, particularly women's clubs; in 1926, she attacked Iowa clubs for tastes in literature that "dulled rather than sharpened the Iowa female brain" (quoted in Ehrhardt 168). Her animus against these institutions, and the popular writers who served them, was personal. She believed that popular women writers fed their readers dangerous lies. Women's very romanticism made them victims; appeals to their emotions made them vulnerable. This connected, as Julia Ehrhardt persuasively argues, with Herbst's bitterness over her own and her sister's unwanted pregnancies and abortions, particularly her sister's death from infection.

Herbst blamed women's novelists and women's magazines for the traps into which she and her sister fell, denouncing the *Ladies' Home Journal* and the *Woman's Home Companion*, by name. In one particularly pointed short story, she contrasts the reality of the small-minded town with the myth of the friendly village: a neighbor day, planned by "Mrs. Gale," clearly a stand-in for the popular novelist Zona Gale, has the theme that "being a neighbor was as universal as having a mother" (quoted in Ehrhardt 122). The friendliness epitomized by Zona Gale's stories doesn't embrace women who choose not to be mothers; Clare cannot find a doctor who will help her end her pregnancy, and in the end she dies from a botched abortion. Herbst's own experiences in Sioux City made her side with Sinclair Lewis against Dorothy Canfield regarding the repressiveness of small-town life.

Though never named, Canfield would have been a target in Herbst's attack on women's magazines and popular women writers. Herbst's two traumatic encounters with abortion happened in 1920 and 1921, just as Canfield published *The Brimming Cup*, her homage to home, family, and children, in the *McCall's* magazine. It is understandable that Herbst would blame women's magazines and their fiction writers for *Kinder, Küche, and Kirche* propaganda: "'The Woman's Home Companion . . . Good Housekeeper [*sic*]. Pretty insipid girls smiled up from the covers, on one a fat baby sprawled, showing two teeth in a wide grin. Everywhere, girls were fixing up to get men; after that came the babies. . . . She was in line, she had to go, she had to march. Left, right, forward, march" (quoted in Ehrhardt 167). Women's magazines controlled and contained women, in Herbst's estimation; thus, she refused to write for them.

Herbst believed that middlebrow authors' activist writing erased women's experiences—like sex out of wedlock, unwanted pregnancy, and abortion—from their fictional universe. In response to the sugary fictional outpouring, she added vinegar, with a dose of strychnine. And yet, her experiences in the twenties were more complicated than her fiction let on. She had wanted to have the child, and changed her mind only under pressure; as Elinor Langer astutely puts it, "both of them accepted as natural that his freedom was worth more than her maternity and that it was his welfare, not hers, that was at stake" (60). Ambivalent about her abortion, she never told her sister about it. When she learned of her sister's death, she cried out, "It's my little sister. I did it" (66). None of this figures in Herbst's novels about her sister in the twenties. She did some significant erasing of her own experiences, simplifying contradictions. It is as if she had to kill off the "romance novel" part of herself to be seen as a "real" writer.

Nor were women's magazines as monochromatic as Herbst suggests—as my discussions of Canfield and Buck indicate. The women's issues Herbst addressed might have been translated for a women's magazine audience, especially in the "new woman" buzz of the 1920s. She would have had to compromise, however, to avoid offending and shocking her audience, and though she would later do just that to hide a lesbian affair, she generally refused this particular compromise as a betrayal of her identity as writer.

Herbst's fervent emotions found other outlets than her writing. She brought an emotional commitment to her politics—an instinctive alliance with the "poor ravaged people of the world" (90)—that contrasted with the cynicism of the twenties and the dogmatism of the thirties. Indeed, her passion for justice placed her in dangerous proximity to the middle-class reformers Mencken and other moderns so despised.

Her authorial identity, then, was split; her hard-edged "modern" realism left out many of her experiences as a woman, as a political activist, and as a daughter of the Midwest. In the early thirties, however, Herbst seemed to have found a national and political ethos that would allow her to merge these three aspects of her personality. That ethos was literary proletarianism.

The Thirties: The Proletarian Novel and Bourgeois Redemption

Proletarian literature[2] has been hotly debated in American letters since its explosion onto the literary scene in the early 1930s. In the first half of the thirties, literary proletarianism was both a Communist-sponsored oppositional practice and a trendy literary phenomenon, one inspired by a cultural shift to the left.[3] Especially in 1934, the year Herbst published *The Executioner Waits*, the proletarian novel was a critical obsession. Periodicals, both mainstream publications like the *Saturday Review* and left-wing magazines like the *New Masses,* discussed proletarian literature in articles, editorials, and book reviews. Publishing houses like Harcourt, Brace, Alfred A. Knopf, and John Day actively sought out proletarian novels, offering advances to struggling writers. Joseph Freeman explained somewhat grumpily in a *New Masses* article in 1934, "The bourgeois publishers think they see a 'market' for left-wing writers. Proletarian literature is all the rage; writers who have been neglected for a decade because they were 'only' Communists are having their books published. No distinctions are made since all that is important is the 'market' " (20). The worker was the new exotic, and this literary trend dominated discussion about literature in 1934. Prestige publishing houses and their often aggressive advertising placed high profile reviews in all the important cultural organs, including the *Saturday Review of Literature* and the *New York Times Book Review.*

Literary proletarianism represented many writers' political awakening. Lincoln Steffens's famous proclamation on the Soviet Union in 1931 that "I have seen the future, and it works" epitomized the hopes of many writers who were horrified by the poverty and class stratification they saw in America. Proletarian novelists hated capitalism for its inequality and exploitation, and not only desired but expected a complete economic transformation. An underlying purpose of their fiction was to persuade their readers of the justice and inevitability of an economic revolution. They wanted to gain a large audience to convert, part of it from a working class that did not read in nearly the same proportion as the middle class. Proletarians thus needed to extend the readership for "serious" fiction and to persuade their readers to use proletarian novels as a guide for political views and social action.

In other words, literary proletarians had a *middlebrow* project, in the sense that Janice Radway has defined it. Many characteristics of literary proletarianism have striking similarities with middlebrow authors' discussion of their craft. Many of their strategies for political engagement—their advocacy of the legitimate role of propaganda and political purpose in fiction, their support for realism and for writing that doesn't alienate the common reader with excessive experimentation, their connection of aesthetic strategies with political goals—echo the strategies of Dorothy Canfield, Jessie Fauset, and Pearl Buck, three reformers whose liberalism and appeals to American "patriotic" values left them out of the emerging critical ethos. In their most famous slogan, "Art is a Class Weapon," literary proletarians identified the political impetus of both highbrow and proletarian literature. That every novel can and should advocate for a more desirable political and social reality was a truism long touted by writers like Canfield, Fauset, and Buck. The relationship between proletarianism and middlebrow is a relationship widely commented on by cold war commentators like Robert Warshow (34–36).

To acknowledge proletarian literature's middlebrow connections, for practitioners and most subsequent critics, is to undermine the validity of the project. Instead of defending literary it from the "charge" of being middlebrow, I want to explore the internal contradictions of proletarian literature that made its instigators disavow their own middlebrow aims.

Proletarian literature, despite its focus on the working class, was always geared toward middle-class readers and writers. With a few notable exceptions (including Mike Gold, Agnes Smedley, and Jack Conroy) practitioners and critics of the proletarian novel came from middle-class backgrounds and had rebelled against their roots in the twenties. The *New Masses*, the Communist-sponsored magazine that became the central vehicle for the movement, targeted the middle class; in 1934 it announced its intended audience as "those in the middle class who have shed their illusions about bourgeois democracy and are ready to fight for a Communist society in alliance with the vanguard of the workers" (Hicks "An Open Letter").

Politically, this middle-class emphasis made sense. The Depression had placed many middle-class people in economic jeopardy and made them vulnerable as the working class had always been vulnerable. As Walter Rideout explains, "When the shock of the Depression dislodged them from a relatively secure economic place in society, they were brought for the first time into angry awareness of social instability, of widespread suffering, and of the violence of industrial dispute" (178). Part of the strategy of left-wing activists was to point out the similarities in experience and build alliances between workers and the lower middle class. Malcolm Cowley recognized the value of this alliance in his 1935 League of American Writers address, "Revolutionary Movement and Writer": "I believe that the interests of my own class lie in a close alliance with the proletariat, and I believe that writers especially can profit by this alliance. . . . Literature and revolution are united not only by their common aim of liberating the human spirit, but also by immediate bonds of interest" (Hart 65). In the 1930s, the middle class was more likely to identify with the lower class than with the upper (McElvaine 223), and Communists wanted to encourage and use this identification to promote revolution. In other words, if middle-class people identified as "proletarian," they would transform American society.

Proletarian writers and critics had a central rhetorical problem, however; they wanted to convert an audience toward which they felt considerable antagonism. They wanted to embrace activism while apparently leaving middle-class progressivism behind. In their shift from cultural to political radicalism, the moderns could keep their disdain for the bourgeoisie intact; they were simultaneously *above* the liberal middle class in their sophisticated radicalism and *beneath* it in their embrace of proletariat, the true impetus behind societal transformation. In both their disdain and their glorification they tried to bypass the hated American middle.

This ambivalence emerges within literary proletarianism in both identity politics and aesthetics. The "working class," for many literary proletarians, was characterized by collective identity, belief, and action—qualities that nineteenth-century Americans would more easily have associated with Christianity. The middle class could only ascend to this powerful working-class collective identity through a mystical conversion. Meridel Le Sueur most succinctly elaborated this religious exaltation of the working class in her 1935 *New Masses* article, "The Fetish of Being Outside." "It is a hard road to leave your own class," she says, "and you cannot leave it by pieces or parts; it is a birth and you have to be born whole out of it. In a complete new body. . . . The creative artist will create no new forms of art or literature for that new hour out of the darkness unless he is willing to go all the way, with full belief, into that darkness" (202). Le Sueur's rhetorical combination of evolutionary progress and mystical conversion enshrines an imaginary, revolutionary working class as the source of grace and salvation.

Le Sueur describes the middle class and the working class as separate species; the working class is the goal toward which the middle class must evolve, losing its ideology as an amphibian loses its gills:

> Everyday I see people rotting, dying in this dead class like plants decaying in a foul soil. I feel I, myself, have rotted and suffered and threshed in this element of the bourgeois class like an organism in a decaying pool with the water evaporating about you the natural elements of your body and desires in stress and your hungers decaying

> and rotting and stinking to high heaven. . . . You cannot grow a fine bloom by equivocation, by only half growing a fine bloom. . . . From these, because of full belief, he will produce a movement, even a miraculous form that has not hitherto existed. Even the lower forms of life are able to step out in this belief into a new element and grow a new orientated fin or organ that makes creative alignments. (202)

Embedded in this Darwinian imagery is materialist progression, which, wedded to Christian conversion, makes for a strange combination. (The idea that "full belief" will cause evolution would have mystified Darwin, for example.) One might argue that Le Sueur's dependence on myths of progress and conversion reveals her profoundly middle-class orientation even as she denies it. More interesting, and troubling for literary proletarianism, is why she felt the need to publicly recant at all. "Real" proletarians like Mike Gold rarely missed an opportunity to let the newly radicalized know that they were, at best, mere assistants to the working-class revolution. An oft-cited debate at the 1934 League of American Writers between Kenneth Burke and Gold shows this dynamic. Burke argued that for maximum rhetorical effectiveness, radicals should replace "workers" with "the people" in their rhetoric (Hart 90); Gold insisted that this would erase the essential working-class character of the movement.

Literary proletarians disavowed the middlebrow and the liberal tradition that underlay so much of middlebrow educational writing and activism.[4] In the *New Masses,* John Dewey was christened the "leading philosopher of the American middle-class" (Lamont 23). His liberalism was seen as merely an excuse to justify existing class relations. Bourgeois liberalism was mocked in articles, reviews, letters to the editor, even a burlesque of middle-class advice columns for "liberals and progressives" focused on their individual love problems.[5]

Aesthetics was another hotly debated topic, one on which proletarians were more concerned with distinguishing themselves from middle-class protest traditions, and with ideological purity, than with actual effects on readers. Realism was the preferred mode. William Dean Howells, the symbol of middle-class euphemism and impotence, was resurrected, with reservations, by none other than Granville Hicks, editor of the *New Masses.* Bernard Smith, in a *Saturday Review* article in 1934, notes the irony: "We may wonder . . . how [Howells's surviving friends] feel on finding in a book by one of the younger Marxists—Granville Hicks's 'The Great Tradition'—a warm and appreciative study of his novels. They are, no doubt, shocked. Howells would not be, if he were alive." Howells's legacy, as Hicks defined it, was the social novel—a focus on the many conflicting, interacting forces in American society. Proletarian fiction eschewed utopian visions for a similar kind of social novel.

The *New Masses,* the preeminent journal of proletarian literature and radical politics, was filled with attacks on esoteric forms of writing and the elitist modernists associated with such writing; such inaccessible experimentalism proved the inevitable bourgeois decay. This attack perhaps reached its height in a satirical interview with Gertrude Stein, in America for a lecture tour in 1935 after the success of *The Autobiography of Alice B. Toklas;* her writing style was used as a symbol of bourgeois irrelevance. By contrast, the *New Masses,* following Moscow's lead, advocated socialist realism, which seemed to have a more intimate and relevant commitment to real life, and had the added benefit of being more accessible to the masses than, say, Stein, James Joyce, or T. S. Eliot. Literary proletarianism's rejection of modernist aesthetics as such, and its commitment to employ realism to attain accessibility and real-world relevance, bears a striking resemblance to the implicit aesthetics of middlebrow writers.

One might assume that Upton Sinclair, one of the best-known and most popular protest novelists of the Progressive era, would have been a respected predecessor to the proletarians, even a role model. But the *New Masses* consistently rejected him as an unskilled propagandist and a "reactionary utopian" (Garlin). His biggest transgression, aside from his overt politics and his embrace of the formal qualities of popular culture, was his insistence on intervention within the current political and economic order. After twice running for governor of California as a socialist, he ran as a Democrat in 1934 under the program "End Poverty in California" (or EPIC), in which he proposed to ease the current economic crisis by having the government take over closed factories to provide secure employment. He appalled the *New Masses* writers with his desire to simultaneously "abolish poverty" and "save capitalism" ("Upton Sinclair's Threat"), for his deferral of the revolution and collapse of capitalism would "inaugurate a system of virtual serfdom, with the workers tied to the land or factories" ("Upton Sinclair's Threat"). Such hyperbolic invective against a writer who was long a champion of the underclass indicates thorough hostility to pragmatic attempts to work within the existing system.

Even more surprisingly, the prototypic writer for the proletarians was not Upton Sinclair but John Dos Passos, whose highly experimental texts were both politically radical and technically advanced. Dos Passos pioneered techniques that other writers in the thirties, including Josephine Herbst, were to adopt as their own. He wrote sprawling, disconnected social novels like the *U.S.A* trilogy, which combined newsreel descriptions, history, brief vignettes of different characters, and autobiography to give a radical impression of a historical period. Dos Passos is a touchstone of sorts in the *New Masses,* and he is proof that one can be both highbrow and radical, advanced aesthetically and politically. His influence at the 1934 American Writers Congress was immense. Nothing better indicates the esteem highbrow aesthetics continued to hold among literary proletarians than Dos Passos's near canonization.

These internal contradictions suggest the "problem" of proletarian literature; it was middlebrow in intention, but disavowed both progressivism and middlebrow authors, its natural allies. For Herbst, in the thick of all these debates through her extensive reportage for the *New Masses* and her participation in the American Writers Congress, these contradictions must have been fraught indeed. As a radical woman writer who focused on the middle class in a trilogy of American life, she was already a step closer to middlebrow and a step further away from mainstream proletarianism. The second installment of her proletarian trilogy, *The Executioner Waits,* was published in 1934, at the height of interest in literary proletarianism, and it casts light on the complicated legacy of proletarian literature.

Herbst's Negotiation of the Marketplace

Herbst, in Julia Ehrhardt's estimation, "was not considered a particularly powerful literary figure by publishers and editors" (141). She lived just on the edge of financial disaster, even in the literary boom of the 1920s, struggling to make her way as a writer, with very little encouragement from mainstream publishing houses. Ehrhardt describes the "plethora of rejection letters stating that the 'drab quality inherent in most of her stories' made it 'difficult' for editors to accept her work" (141). It isn't surprising that she made her struggle a virtue. Unlike many of her fellow writers, Herbst really believed in the role of the struggling artist, instead of just embracing it as a temporary strategy. By the end of her writing career, she had become a nun of sorts to the craft, her struggle a sign of her superior talent and insight, her unwillingness to sell out.

Despite Herbst's rejections from more solvent publishers, however, she negotiated the marketplace much more effectively than Jessie Fauset, using personal and political connections. She circulated her writing privately among friends, and had a reputation among modern writers. This modern version of patronage had its rewards, as did her drinking in Paris and fishing in Key West with Hemingway. Her network of modern writers may not have made Herbst rich, but it had tangible advantages in publishing. British modernist Ford Madox Ford helped her find her first publisher; Ernest Hemingway and Ring Lardner provided jacket blurbs; Katherine Anne Porter reviewed her positively (Langer 101). With these modern credentials, Herbst's first novel was "reviewed in at least fifty newspapers" (101).

Herbst's fledgling publisher Coward-McCann, which had begun operations in 1928, further cemented her relationship with cultural and political radicals. Coward-McCann also published Agnes Smedley's *Daughter of Earth* in 1929, and was a decidedly modern, even radical, publishing house. Additionally, Helen Black (Mike Gold's lover) worked there; she passed on inside information about sales and advances, which helped Herbst procure advances to write full-time (Black Letter to Herbst 4 December 1928). Herbst's agent, Maxim Lieber, was an avowed Communist who worked with her husband John Herrman as a spy in the mid-thirties (Langer 157).

Herbst had excellent access to periodicals as well, as both a fiction writer and a journalist. She didn't write for the *Saturday Evening Post* or *Scribner's* or even the *Nation*, but she did publish short stories and features for little magazines like *transition* and the *New Masses*, and occasional articles for the slightly more mainstream *American Mercury* and the *New Republic*. Her modern connections gave her a control over her authorial identity out of proportion to her actual readership. There were no Dorothy Canfield–esque audiences and advances, but she had outlets for books, stories, and articles in smaller presses. Her New York connections guaranteed the means to print, if not a large audience.

For a writer who had made disregarding, even outraging, the middlebrow a virtue, Herbst was in a curious position in the early thirties, one shared by her newly converted radical compatriots. She suddenly wanted to reach a broader middle-class audience. Her apprenticeship in her transformation to politically committed writing came through journalism; the *New Masses* provided an excellent forum for her political writing, especially in 1934 when it actively sought intellectuals and the disaffected among the middle class. Herbst's political and economic education was enhanced by her diligence, her bravery, and her aptitude for being at the right place at the right time. She had visited Russia in 1930 for the International Writer's Conference, as scores of Americans were praising the Bolshevik experiment; she attended a convention of small farmers very like the ones she grew up with, radicalized by the Depression and the New Deal's favoritism toward wealthy landowners; she traveled to Cuba and gained access to radical organizers in hiding in 1934; she reported on the hunted resistance to Hitler in Germany in 1935; and, in an encounter that haunted her for the rest of her life, she spent three months in the Civil War in Spain, a rite of passage for a whole generation of writers, including Hemingway, Sylvia Townsend Warner, John Dos Passos, and W. H. Auden. Of Spain, Herbst wrote nearly thirty years later, "In the most real sense my most vital life did indeed end with Spain. Nothing so vital, either in my personal life or in the life of the world, has ever come again" (quoted in Langer x). These political involvements sharpened for Herbst the power of the left-wing critique she had embraced.

Marxist economic analysis also influenced her major literary project of the thirties, a proletarian trilogy. Growing up in Iowa, Herbst had been raised on stories of her poor uncle Joe, a carpetbagger after the Civil War who spent his life searching for fortune and ended up insane and penniless. She also had witnessed her parents' endless quest for security, constantly thwarted by circumstance. Through her shift left, she suddenly understood the logic underlying her family's constant disappointments. Herbst had rejected her middle-class background and embraced modernist rebellion; but she had always kept "unrealistic" ideals about justice and equality at the heart of her radicalism. She gravitated toward noble lost causes in the late twenties and thirties—American farmers' militant protest, Cuban resistance, German resistance to Hitler, and the Spanish Civil War. These all reflected a kind of ideal community, a city on a hill that was usually in danger of being destroyed by big business or fascist violence. Her political rebellions, in other words, were inflected through American ideals and idioms.

This passionate radicalism gave Herbst's middle-class background back to her in the thirties as something to be valued and understood, not despised. Her proletarian trilogy—*Pity Is Not Enough, The Executioner Waits, Rope of Gold*—reinterpreted her family story. She understood her parents' struggle, their futile belief in the American dream and their inability to achieve it, as part of a larger pattern. It wasn't that their ideals were wrong, but that they were incapable of achieving them in an America that had been hijacked by big business. "Communism is twentieth-century Americanism," a slogan Communist party president Earl Browder introduced in 1934, expressed the focus on radicalism's American-ness that would become the hallmark of the Popular Front in the late thirties. Herbst decided to depict in fiction the hopelessness and inevitable decline of American culture under industrialism by telling the story of a "typical" middle-class American family to show how their lives, like those of the working class, were controlled and blighted by capitalism.

Her shift in focus, perfectly timed to meet literary trends, led to new clout with publishers. At first, the decision seemed disastrous; her press balked at her new project. Coward-McCann had been supportive for Herbst's first two novels, and it wanted to continue as her publisher. But faced with a worsening economy, the press wasn't excited about her Marxist trilogy. Editor Tom Conrad rejected *Pity Is Not Enough* because "the absence of any inflection in such a long book is apt to give the reader . . . a sense of monotony. I doubt," he concluded, "this novel's success from a purely commercial standpoint" (Maxim Lieber Letter to Herbst 22 November 1932). She had a completed novel without a publisher.

Herbst and her agent turned this setback into her biggest literary coup to date. Agent Maxim Lieber negotiated a three-book contract from Harcourt, Brace, and Co. This was a clear step up the publishing-world staircase. By the early thirties, Harcourt, Brace had firmly established its reputation as the publisher of John Dos Passos, Sinclair Lewis, Dorothy Canfield, John Maynard Keynes, Lytton Strachey, Virginia Woolf, and other authors engaged in modern debates. It had influence, money for advances, and effective marketing staff. And it was enthusiastic about Herbst's writing. That they carried her for nearly two years, offering "to give you a contact for your next book, sight unseen, to show you the confidence they had in your work" (Lieber Letter to Herbst 1 June 1931), reveals Harcourt's savvy in anticipating and helping to build the coming trend for "proletarian" fiction.

Harcourt backed up its enthusiasm with concrete assistance. They gave

Herbst a $750 advance to allow her to work full-time on the second installment in the trilogy. (Fauset, by contrast, had received a $100 advance from Boni & Liveright in the booming twenties.) The firm also promised, as Lieber explained, "to put out a substantial advertising campaign for the novel and you will be in on consultations regarding such promotion if you choose" (Lieber Letter to Herbst 22 November 1932). Herbst, in other words, was promised support and control over her public image. This was a world apart from the familial rapport of Helen Black at Coward-McCann; Herbst was in the big leagues.

She also found a supportive and savvy editor in Charles Pearce. Pearce consulted with her carefully about reviewers and jacket blurbs, and inquired about missed deadlines in the gentlest possible way (Letter to Josephine Herbst 5 July 1933; 11 October 1933). If Herbst didn't enjoy the intimacy that Canfield and Buck had with their publishers, she had a very competent and sympathetic advocate within Harcourt Brace—one she shared with John Dos Passos.

Herbst took advantage of this newfound influence with the publication of *Pity Is Not Enough*, consulting with Pearce about the design of the jacket cover (Pearce Letter to Herbst 20 December 1933) and approving the new jacket. Sales had reached about 1,400 by December 1934 (Pearce Letter to Herbst 14 December 1934). But the book's reviews, plentiful and praiseful, showed the benefits of Herbst's new liaison. *Pity Is Not Enough* was recommended in the *Book-of-the-Month Club News* as a promising novel (Pearce Letter to Herbst 25 March 1933). A broader middlebrow audience seemed within reach.

It was the second installment of the trilogy, which brought the saga of the Trexlers into the present, that most excited Harcourt, Brace. Charles Pearce pushed Herbst to finish by the spring of 1934 to capitalize on the first novel's visibility and the media attention surrounding literary proletarianism:

> I have been talking with Maxim Lieber about THE EXECUTIONER WAITS AT THE DOOR. I am sorry that it has been necessary for you to delay work on it to do a few magazine articles, etc., and hoped that you would be able to make a further advance on the novel at this time, in order that you might be free to finish it for spring publication. However, I have discovered that our salesmen would much rather be selling the book next fall than next spring. They'd like at

> least a year between publication of the two novels, and since PITY IS NOT ENOUGH came out so late in May, it would be impossible for us to publish it before September if we were to allow a full year to intervene. Moreover, they believe that the chance of doing big things with EXECUTIONER will be better next fall. (Pearce Letter to Herbst 11 October 1933)

Pearce provided Herbst with a particularly astute education in the logistics of publishing; she had every reason to be enthusiastic about finding a large audience ready to be persuaded by her radical conversion.

Moderns, Proletarians, and Middle Class Decay: *The Executioner Waits*

In her trilogy, Herbst made her political awakening a uniquely American phenomenon. "Most of the energizing forces for the left," she wrote a student in the Sixties, "came from old American virtues" (Letter to Monty Penkower 18 December 1967). To show that radicalism indeed came from "old American virtues," Herbst focused mainly on the middle class, deriving her conclusions from their experience alone. *The Executioner Waits* focuses on the twentieth century from World War I until the Crash, pursuing the Trexler family's saga into economic insecurity and cultural breakdown.

Harcourt, Brace enthusiastically advertised this novel. It solicited for "puffs" from sympathetic writers, eliciting this lighthearted response from Erskine Caldwell, a radical Southern writer:

> Josephine Herbst has written an honest-to-goodness American book, a thing that very few writers can do. *The Executioner Waits* is the goal that most writers set out to reach when they attempt to tell the story of a family; the influence of American life on people has rarely been so well interpreted before. P.S. Hello, you lechers at Harcourt, Brace, I'm glad you have published a good book for a change. (Caldwell Letter to Harcourt, Brace undated)

Caldwell's insistence that Herbst had written an "American" book supports Jennifer Parchesky's contention that the middle class was becoming the symbol of typical American-ness. His praise of her portrait of family and American life set the tone for the reviews that followed publication.

Harcourt, Brace equated "middle class" and "American" seamlessly in their advertising, capitalizing upon the novel's subject matter skillfully in an 18 September 1934 issue of *Harcourt, Brace News:*

> She has spread on a huge canvas the lives of a middle class family. They are not the rich people, they are not the working class, but the *backbone people of the American nation.* . . . They are the solid folk who talk in terms of American traditions, who feel that they must own their own houses and that their children must be alive to "opportunities" which will come to them as their deserved American birthright. What happens to these children, what in the way of ideals and ambitions they take into the world, what frustrations and what happinesses they find, what makes them, as many writers have termed it, the "lost generation" is a dominating theme of the novel—perhaps a corollary to the central idea of the disintegration of the middle class. (*Harcourt, Brace News,* italics added)

In the publisher's implied ideology, the rich and the working class are too extreme to represent American-ness. Harcourt, Brace was convinced that Herbst could capture the full attention of the middle-class reading public. Published shortly after Malcolm Cowley's memoir *Exile's Return,* Herbst's novel was advertised to benefit from the widespread re-evaluation of the twenties that Cowley's memoir inspired.

Book reviewers hailed *The Executioner Waits* as a major achievement. Indeed, all of the publicity generated by advertising and reviews led to rumors (carefully fostered by Harcourt, Brace) that the novel was a serious contender for the Pulitzer Prize (Langer 161). Horace Gregory proclaimed that "the publication of this second volume established her right to be considered one of few major novelists in America today" (4). The emphasis on "America" is key. Herbst's focus on middle-class Americans, or "real" Americans, comes up in numerous reviews; one sees the characters as "symbols of middle-class America" (Review *Waldorf-Astoria*). Many reviewers found Herbst, like Dorothy Canfield, an insightful and sympathetic interpreter of middle-class life.

Their commentary assumed that reviewers, readers, and publishers are just like the white, middle-class Americans Herbst describes. One review opens with questions: "What is happening to all good middle-class folk upon whom all the Jeffersonian principles of free self-determination and self government are based? Are we still the backbone of the nation?" (Review *Opinion*). The unconscious shift from "good middle-class folk" to "we" shows how naturally the reviewer assumed his audience; he also uses Harcourt, Brace's promotional materials in his own review, revealing both his malleability and the advertisement's effectiveness. Another review asserted, "You will recognize your friends and relatives in this novel. . . . You will even have to recognize yourself in some character" (Review *Common Sense*). A third review proclaimed enthusiastically, "Here is the kind of writing which will make thousands of housewives, business men, and their children exclaim, 'This is about me!'. . . Josephine Herbst knows us, the American middle-class, almost better than we know ourselves, and her fierce but friendly insight makes her irresistible" (Review *Salden*).

The Executioner Waits focuses on businessmen, housewives, young rebels, farmers, and radicals. Like Dos Passos's fiction, it interweaves a number of narratives, alternating between the older and the younger generation of Trexlers, but also focusing on the Chance family, whose son Jonathan becomes involved with Victoria Trexler midway through the novel. The older generation includes David Trexler, a vain capitalist, his mousy wife, and her spinster sister Millie; Abel Chance, a self-righteous miser, and his avaricious, son-obsessed wife; Anne Trendel, sister of David and always desperately seeking to get ahead, and her husband Amos, who having failed in business is working at great economic insecurity; and Aaron Trexler, a dying skinflint who fleeces Anne and is being fleeced by his wife and son in turn. The younger generation includes David Trexler's children, both of whom are kept under his thumb, the son by working for him, the daughter by a spinsterhood caused by David's interference in a courtship; Jonathan Chance, the free-spirited son of the Chances, and his modern friends in Detroit; and Anne Trexler's daughters, especially Victoria and Rosamond, who wander, lost, through the American landscape. Herbst follows their lives from the Progressive era and World War I through the Crash, interspersing their personal stories with contemporary vignettes of social and economic unrest. But the unifying theme of these often loosely connected scenes and narratives is the hopeless decline of the middle class. To Herbst middle-class culture (the white is, of course, implicit) has three main characteristics: sacred symbols and homilies; faith in the work ethic, individualism, and the power of poverty; and adherence to respectability and decorum. By showing the bankruptcy of each of these bourgeois qualities, Herbst moves her readers left.

For twentieth-century Progressives like Canfield, Fauset, and Buck, Christianity was a necessary fiction for social progress, meaningful but not "true" in any literal sense. For Herbst's middle class, secular Christianity has degenerated into meaningless drivel and hypocritical self-justification and self-righteousness. Though many of the men's names come from the Bible—Abel, Aaron, and David—the characters are greedy, not righteous. The few who devoutly believe are misfits, and perhaps charlatans. As Amos thinks of the mayor, "There was something doubtful about a fellow who had been a preacher in a regular church. . . . He still talked the language of the pews and it was Amos' experience that the majority didn't think anymore about religion than he did" (113). The mayor's subsequent betrayal of the IWW proves Amos's suspicions (133).

For most of the older generation in *The Executioner Waits*, Christianity has become simply a status symbol. Jonathan Chance's father, Abel, has abandoned the angst-ridden search for salvation that characterized his forebears: "Abel Chance did not worry about his soul. As a deacon of the church his soul was taken care of. . . . He would as soon think of not winding his watch as of not going to church" (216). Protestant Christianity, as in Max Weber's famous analysis, undergirds capitalism, promoting dependability, order, and control. Indeed, Christianity is the final means for concealing the ugliness of capitalism. At the end of his life, Aaron Trexler listens to his father's prosaic journal of exploring and punctuates it with Scripture. His sister Anne is "terrible disturbed to hear him quote scripture," because

> She had seen nothing in his letters to show that he had gone back on his old atheistic beliefs. It was a shock to hear him now, worse than if a believer had begun swearing on his death bed that there was no god. . . . To have Aaron speak religion was a living decay. . . . She despised her brother for his weakness and hoped he would not ask her to read to him again. He had taken up religion, it was clear as day, because he had long ago given up the world. . . . He had laid his hand on his wife, and on everyone, wilfully, to do what he liked, and when he had finished, he had taken up God. (63–64)

For Aaron, God is the one figure left to manipulate without repercussions. Dependence on Scripture is one sign of the "decay" of the middle class; God has become so powerless in middle-class culture that he is just another person to exploit.

For the older generation in *The Executioner Waits,* Christianity has ceased to be a sustaining myth. After her daughter's death, Anne Wendel longs for its assurance and knows that she cannot have it. Other myths stand in as poor substitutes for this faith. The Home is one such myth. The IWW endangers American life because, the newspaper reports, "the purposes of the I.W.W. are to proclaim free love . . . [and] to disrupt the greatest American institution, the Home" (145). Even Anne, as "modern" as she tries to be, tries to persuade Victoria to marry by sending her platitudes about the values of family and home. David Trexler confidently proclaims, "This country is founded on home building. . . . It's the rock on which we stand. Without homes we'd be a wasted migratory lot, without roots. Save, that's number one, number two is to buy a home" (266). Trexler's shift from the ideology of Home to home as property demonstrates how enmeshed values are in capitalism.

Education is another myth of the middle class: "Education was a fine thing, it lasted when money failed you. Even when health deserted you, you had it" (156). When led into doubts by "some of the slighting things Vicky said about [education]," Anne Wendel longs for her Emerson or Thoreau (156) to steady her. Genteel faith in the democratic and ennobling power of education, a faith that fueled middlebrow institutions in the twenties and thirties, comes under assault in the novel. Both Home and Education connect with middle-class faith in uplift and upward mobility, but they also serve a quasi-religious function.

When these symbols fail, there are disconnected homilies, poems, and sayings that appear to give order and meaning to the chaos of living. Various middle-class characters, including the boarding house keeper and leaders of business, dismiss strikers with the same mantra, "Liberty was one thing, license was another" (100), and this phrase never fails to justify the repression of labor. In Victoria's room is a framed "motto" about the value of solitude and its ability to lead one to God. For Herbst, all such middle-class value systems are emotionally as well as materially inadequate.

The emptiness of these values doesn't prevent them from controlling the older generation and dogging the younger. Inane homilies dictate behavior. Decorum and respectability restrict and control even without the religious beliefs that once justified them. At a respectable home,

> The curious superior way they talked seemed old-fashioned. Victoria looked around wondering if she could slip out and go home. But no, she was a Family Friend, and so sat while the cake was cut. KEEP OUT KEEP OFF THE GRASS PRIVATE PROPERTY KEEP OFF SHOOT EVERY LIVING THING and with her arm around Lilly's waist she sang with the rest of them. (44)

Rules abound, particularly that no one, especially women, should say anything controversial. These justify a repressive system based on property. Violence undergirds respectability; violations of property—including land, machinery, and women—may be punished by "shooting every living thing." Middle-class proprieties, like Victoria's responsibility as a Family Friend to be a Nice Girl, value property over actual people.[6]

Herbst goes further: loosening rules of sexual conduct for women, she implies, outrages people because it lessens women's property value. Herbst reveals this connection in the unreflecting rant of a boarding house keeper in Seattle, who is appalled at the freedom of Victoria and Rosamond Wendel:

> She felt sometimes as if immorality was going on right at the table when those two girls would start at it, bold as brass, criticizing the world. . . . Oh what a high-handed way to do things. You'd think they'd show some discretion. The way the war made girls carry on was a caution. If it wasn't running outright with men, it was flaunting opinions that did credit to no decent woman, right in the faces of a whole table of the young and innocent. Why they had the nerve, those girls, to laugh at what everyone knows is true; everyone knows that the revolution was just to nationalize women, so as to give them license. (100)

Intellectual, political, and sexual promiscuity become hopelessly intertwined in Mrs. Caspar's muddled thinking. The real goal of radicals is to "nationalize women," that is, to abolish private property in women and to make them collective property, of the state. Faced with these two alternatives, Mrs. Caspar prefers being private property. Her defense of the system is curious; she has been abandoned by her husband and gains neither economic nor social benefits from the title "Mrs." But, Herbst demonstrates, such slavish devotion to decorum makes capitalism function.

Small-time capitalists like David Trexler and Abel Chance succeed through hypocrisy and lack of character. Upward mobility ignores the decent, like Amos Wendel, and rewards insecure and contemptible petty tyrants. David Trexler, for example, promotes "fair business practices" while refusing to help his own sister in need. He doesn't help "out of respect for her. . . . Independence and the exercise of individual initiative were the foundations on which this country had risen to first rank, and he had risen also and hoped he used his means wisely and with due regard to the laws of nature" (297). Abel Chance refuses to pay for Victoria to go to her mother's deathbed for similar reasons; he uses her distress as an excuse to berate Jonathan for being an inadequate provider. Under all these clichés lies manipulative greed.

The youth rebellion of the twenties, Herbst suggests, rises from the same economic sources as the rebels' genteel parents' ennui. Middle-class life, with its antiquarian homilies and self-abusive values, no longer seems real. Victoria longs for "something *real.* For love, like she could feel in her bones existed somewhere, for something that took you along like a great river" (96). Gus envies his brother in the IWW, for when "you see Ed, you'll think you've missed living" (111). Anne Trexler, learning covertly of Victoria's affair with a married man, knows she should be scandalized, but "her girl was experiencing life, she was living" (206). Victoria and Jonathan envy their friends in Europe their vivid experiences. Victoria longs for meaning, thinking that "it would be a consolation to die for a cause that would go on, forever" (276).

All that is left, for both the older and the younger generation, is pity and sentimentality. Sentiment, though, is the opiate of the middle class, thoroughly irrelevant to the reality of their lives. David Trexler's self-absorption prevents him from true empathy with others. As a young man, he wanted to run off with an actress, and still regrets not going, yet he prevents his sister-in-law from doing the same kind of thing, and glories over her taking the best years of her life in spinsterly service. He pities himself as a poor, misunderstood orphan; remembering his father, he murmurs " 'What a pity,'. . . sorry for himself, the fatherless child" (363). Even in his self-pity, self-interest is paramount. Vicky offers him family letters for free that he had been scheming to buy at a low price, and he rewards her by leaving a five-dollar bill, instead of the ten he had been planning to spend, pinned to her pillow (367). He is angry at being deceived by his wife's sister Millie, who loves another man, but feels no sorrow for Millie's twenty years of pining.

The younger generation may deplore such sentimentality, but they are no less individualistic and trivial. In their hard-edged rejection of sentiment, they are no less controlled by it. Jonathan and his friends disdain the "booboisie" as "a class who bought the wrong pictures, ate mediocre food, read the worst books" and "made love in the most boring way" (100), but they don't discuss political or economic questions. Those like Victoria, more attuned to the contradictions, are sick of pity: "everywhere talk and pity, pity, until it made her feel as hard as nails" (95). The pity comes instead of meaningful action, as Victoria learns after her mother dies. After "it was too late," Hortense and David send flowers, but "pity could not help her" (337).

Herbst doesn't simply dismiss middle-class people; she makes sense of their helplessness. The problem is that only bold action, not sentiment, can transform capitalism. Sentiment, ideals, even love—all are meaningless in such a society. Victoria has learned this from her carpetbagger Uncle Joe:

> The world was still full of young hopeful men, who like Uncle Joe, turned and twisted hoping for fortunes. All their good generous qualities were in danger of trapping them, not helping them, in a world where the plums went to the biggest thieves. Money, money, money makes the mare go, was one of her father's sayings that came from dear knows where. It was a kind of crime not to want money and only money. (313)

Pithy slogans about business are totally false; theft, violence, duplicity, and avarice are the keys to success, not integrity and hard work.

And capitalism's influence, Herbst shows, is not confined to the marketplace. It corrupts the Home, by causing jealousy and bad feeling. Both Victoria and Rosamond are jealous of their mother's expenditures on the house. Anne steals two pieces of property from Aaron, who is so greedy that he has made Anne beg for food money even as, through her help,he has saved on the cost of a nurse. Jonathan's mother punishes her son by "starv[ing] them out" (349). Anne and her sister Hortense quarrel bitterly over eight dollars: "a kind of frenzy was in her sister, all the injustices heaped upon her during a lifetime of petty storekeeping raged now at Anne" (311). It corrupts marriage, making it simply an economic transfer. It makes the very land the Home is built on unstable; when David Trexler argues that "Real estate is something that no one can take away," his nephew-in-law "would have answered that even the ground can slip from under your feet if you can't pay taxes" (361).

Having established middle-class life as a prison, Herbst provides only one solution—working-class culture. The betrayed middle class needs to make alliances with the dispossessed, not with those who exploit it. Such coalitions will provide meaning, power, and "real life." Victoria longs "for something that took you along like a great river" (97); Rosamond remarks, after singing with the IWW, that "it would be fine to sing like that with hundreds, with thousands of people" (154). Trapped in middle-class individualism, they can discern no means of escape; through contacts with workers, they discover new faith. Jerry Stauffer finds a solution through participating in the strike and identifying with the workers: "Not since they had grabbed him into the army from Rosamond had he felt so lighthearted. The war hadn't been his war, but he hadn't known how to get out of it. He could get out of this. He was getting out. He got out into the clear cold air" (238). Jerry ultimately decides that "he wouldn't be foolish and try to rise on someone else's neck, he'd stay down, right here with his own people until someday they could all rise together" (286). Jonathan finally discovers in Marx the words to explain his life; living in Pennsylvania "his mind's eye knew that the clue was buried in the very farms around him. He could realize a pattern, the system that was creating topheavy wealth for the few and misery for the many" (316). When discussing the chaos of modern life with David Trexler, he explains that "maybe people still had plenty of faith only none in the old faiths" (362). They realize that "Uncle David belonged to another country; she and Jonathan belonged here surrounded by people who had no more than they did" (363). Like Canfield's characters in *The Brimming Cup,* those in *The Executioner Waits* find meaning in activism, but activism demands radical change.

Herbst provides direct commentary on this 1920s story in Dos Passos–like "interchapters" that flash forward to detail conditions in 1934. One narrator describes a "bunch of old Mennonites and Dutchies" in

Doylestown, "a good old town that belong to William Penn," singing the International with upraised fists" (353–354). Under the previous moral for the neighborhood, written on a big rock, "PREPARE TO MEET THY GOD," an activist writes a new one: "WORKERS OF THE WORLD UNITE" (352). One New Dealer, trying to avert disaster, works to keep farmers, storekeepers, and farmhands apart, for "if they ever realized they were in the same boat, if they ever quit tearing at each other's throats, if the little storekeeper ever got it into his head that his friend, his only friend was the poor farmer, not the rich banker, where in hell would the system be then?" (215). The novel ends with the promise of such a coalition, but as yet, all that is assured is the irrelevance of bankers like David Trexler, who tries to intimidate a crowd of strikers and is ignored, and sees a vision of his own grave.

By defining the middle class as bankrupt individualists, Herbst constructs a fictional world so hopeless that only the collective, virile working class and radical politics provide redemption. Her novel's eventual influence, however, was not what she had hoped.

"Emotion and Tenderness and Mother Love": Herbst and Resistance to Female Middlebrow Authorship

The Executioner Waits seemed to be uniquely poised for commercial success. It was timely, it was published by a prestigious and supportive publishing house, it benefited from extensive advertising, and it was reviewed positively, and in all the right places, including the *New York Times Book Review,* the *Saturday Review of Literature,* and the *Book-of-the-Month Club News.* But it did not become a best seller; Herbst, like Fauset, struggled to build an audience large enough to support herself.

Herbst's editor had his own theories why. Hoping to capitalize on the trend of the proletarian novel, Harcourt, Brace had rushed *The Executioner Waits* into print for the 1934 fall season. Because Herbst took longer to finish than expected, the novel wasn't published until October 25. In a 1938 letter regarding the publication of *Rope of Gold,* Charles Pearce, her editor, wrote to her about the difficulties that this rushed publication caused:

> We're all unhappy that *The Executioner* came through so late in the fall season. It didn't have the benefits of a full season's promotion

> and publicity, in spite of Miss Taylor's energetic advertising campaign. It came out much too close to the Christmas season. . . . We now believe it extremely important to have complete books in our hands at least one month before publication date. (Letter to Herbst 29 July 1938)

Pearce's explanation was practical. The issue seems more complicated, however. Harcourt, Brace's carefully planned release of *Rope of Gold,* which was delayed for over a year from the date of the above letter, didn't result in large sales. *Rope of Gold,* of course, was published after the proletarian furor had subsided. But *The Grapes of Wrath* and *Native Son* both sold well at that time.

The larger issue may be the internal contradictions of literary proletarianism. Proletarians disavowed any similarities between their own project and the work of Dewey, Canfield, Buck, and Fauset; to do so would suggest that the middle class wasn't just a "ruined," outmoded group sure to wither away in the face of working-class culture. But their aesthetic disdain for the kinds of writing that the working class actually did read guaranteed that they would find neither middle-class readers nor working-class readers. The working class, romanticized as the salvation of American culture, replaced the New Negro as the new exotic for many modern writers. These young converts refused to acknowledge the working class as they actually were; hence, they floundered in their search for readers. Hardly anyone, proletarian or not, bought proletarian novels. Henry Hart explained in 1935 at the American Writers Congress that the consensus was quickly growing that "proletarian and revolution novels don't sell" (Hart 161). He provided the following statistics as evidence:

> Bernard Smith, the editor of Knopf's, recently gathered some figures on the sales of novels by revolutionary writers. These figures, from the publisher's point of view, that is, from the standpoint of profit, are very bad. Now it requires a sale of about 2,000 copies for a publisher to get back what he invested—before he makes anything. Cantwell's *Land of Plenty* had the largest sale—3,000 copies. Jack Conroy's *The Disinherited* sold 2,700, but of these 1,000 were sold at a considerably reduced discount. William Rollins' fine novel *The Shadow Before* has not sold 1,200. Novels which all of you know, and have read, and admired, have sold less than 1,000 copies. (Hart 161)

Even *New Masses*' subscribers slighted proletarian novels. Subscriptions to the magazine jumped from 6,000 in 1933 to 25,000 by the end of 1934 (Rideout 150); it was as high as 100,000 in 1937. If the average proletarian novel sold only 1,000 copies, then even the most generous estimate shows less than 5 percent of its readership supporting popular fiction.

Louis Adamic, in an exposé published in the *Saturday Review* in 1934, argued that, whoever might actually buy proletarian literature, the workers were not among them (322). In his yearlong investigation, he learned that most workers found proletarian literature overly difficult and inauthentic, and they preferred more entertaining, accessible writing. Building on Adamic's article, Erin Smith argues that pulp fiction, particularly hard-boiled detective fiction, not "proletarian literature," was the true fiction of the masses.

This is not to say, of course, that literary Marxists, materialists that they were, didn't consider questions of audience and access at all. The *New Masses* contains many very insightful articles about the publishing industry, including a fascinating critique of the evolution of the *American Mercury*, and Henry Hart, recognizing the problem of sales, proposed a book club that seemed to be organized along the lines of the Book-of-the-Month Club. But what the literary proletarians didn't do satisfactorily was consider the kind of writing they were producing. Proletarian critics' unwillingness to question "natural" categories of "literary merit" prevented proletarian fiction from reaching any actual proletarians. By rejecting middlebrow writing strategies, including identification and a reading experience that both affirmed and challenged, they were unable to achieve their middlebrow aims. Proletarian literature's disavowal of the middlebrow, liberalism, and middle-class values prevented it from reaching a broad audience among any class.

This is particularly germane when considering Herbst's career in the interwar period. She worked for Mencken's wildly successful pulp empire, and saw the kinds of fiction that appealed to working-class readers. She dismissed this as trash. She objected to women's magazines as well, for the lies she believed they told and the emotion they used to sell them. In 1929, Herbst sent the *New Masses* a letter complaining that publishers wanted only "EMOTION AND TENDERNESS AND MOTHER LOVE" (Langer 100). Herbst's relationship to the use of emotion continued to be a key issue in her writing, as were her fraught relationships to women's novels and middlebrow authorship.

An even larger issue was readerly identification. Middlebrow culture always combined pleasing readers and educating them, but for Herbst, as for Fauset, education trumped identification. The more effectively Herbst created a middlebrow reading experience—the more she emphasized "EMOTION AND TENDERNESS AND MOTHER LOVE"—the more she reinforced characteristics she wanted to eradicate.

The Book-of-the-Month Club, both in its published reviews and in informal reader reports, may provide a useful litmus test for determining the effect of Herbst's prose on middlebrow readers. A review published in the November 1934 *Book-of-the-Month Club News* indicates the club's reserve about formal choices in *The Executioner Waits:*

> This is an oddly written book. It can hardly be said to be constructed at all. . . . Nothing holds it together except the characters and their family interest in one another. Indeed, in many ways, *The Executioner Waits,* like the first part of the novel which preceded it, reminds one of a bundle of family letters out of an old chest in the attic.

It is extremely suggestive that the Book-of-the-Month Club was criticizing Herbst's apparent formlessness. She here experienced individually what literary proletarianism suffered collectively. That her particular formlessness is envisioned as a "bundle of family letters" indicates that gender is also a factor. BOMC defined their reservations about Herbst in terms of literary merit.

Privately, however, the club's reviewers found her formal strategies troubling because they hindered general readers from identifying fully with the main characters.[7] They insisted that there be central characters and complained that there were too many major and minor characters. One report for the third novel in Herbst's trilogy, *Rope of Gold,* complains that the reader "is constantly being let down on the very point of believing in" Victoria and Jonathan, the two characters whose experience should guide the reader's own political conversion" (Reader Report *Rope of Gold*). Herbst tries to prevent readers from identifying too strongly with any one character, to emphasize the impotence and ultimate unimportance of the individual, but this may also prevent the reader from feeling sympathy for the "ruined middle class" and their hopelessness. As the second reader of *Rope of Gold* explains, "This book, in spite of its weakness, should interest many patient readers but I feel that it would delight, exalt, engross, stimulate, excite or even simply interest very few who lack the virtue of patience" (Reader Report *Rope of Gold*). An exemplary middlebrow reading experience, these reports implicitly argue, is passionate engagement, and this text, at least for these readers, inhibited their ability to have such an experience. Herbst was writing to transform her readers, particularly to replace their obsession with their individual experience with a larger, structural critique. For proletarian writers, optimism and especially sympathy were questionable, foolish, and hopelessly middle-class. While sympathetic to many of her characters— especially Anne Wendel, the mother figure—Herbst does not want readers to identify with them too strongly. Part of the point of her novel is that these characters are fundamentally wrong in their understanding of the world.

Gender further complicated her relationship to sentiment. Mike Gold might be able to write of dramatic conversions and obsessive mother-love in *Jews without Money*, but he was both a man and a "real" proletarian who had encouraged other men to "go Left" into a masculinized proletarianism. Herbst, as a middle-class woman, could easily be made into a symbol of effeminate liberalism; she knew that such a designation would prevent critics and writers from taking her seriously. She consequently wrote in spare, almost cold prose, a style that contrasts strikingly with her passionate love letters to Marion Greenwood.

This repression of emotion, however, didn't lead reviewers or readers to treat her as one of the boys. A review in the *Carolina Magazine* faults Herbst for thinking too much without feeling: "As a thinking novel, Miss Herbst's is well up near the top of the season's list. As a feeling novel it must take lower rank. When she succeeds in whipping down this all-fired coldness, she may be expected to be one of the truly distinguished novelists of this generation" (Review *Carolina Magazine*). That "all-fired coldness" exempts her from the ranks of "truly distinguished novelists," but the "all-fired coldness" of, say, Ernest Hemingway didn't prevent him from claiming a central role in thirties' literary culture. Only convention, perhaps, prevents the *Carolina Magazine* reviewer from stating his real objection and calling Herbst "frigid." Too much emotion gets women writers dismissed as sentimental; Dorothy Canfield, Jessie Fauset, and Pearl Buck had both their writing and their political commitments dismissed with just such knowing comments. One letter to the *New Masses* praised Herbst for her "kitchen-insight into feminine psychology" (Hicks 25). Too little emotion fails liberate Herbst from the category of "woman writer," even, or especially, among her fellow radicals. Her style makes her, rather, an unnatural woman writer.

And yet Herbst's writing persona relied on themes and concerns of women's novels—the focus on family dynamics; love and its failure; inopportune deaths; despair; genealogy and the epic sweep and decline of a prototypically American family. Despite her rejection, or inversion, of *how* women writers treat such topics, she participates in these middle-class feelings in spite of herself. Middle-class convention—regarding abortion, "normal" sex lives, and family values—inhibited middle-class readers from recognizing these similarities. One of the BOMC readers explained his reticence: "I missed the softening humor of a writer like Irwin Shaw, who really likes his characters, and felt that although the sardonic treatment of all characters, left and right, lent balance to the book, it weakened its value as a plea for a particular way of life" (Reader Report *Rope of Gold*). Readers were unaccustomed to such harsh criticism in their middlebrow experience.

Like Fauset's, Herbst's mode of middlebrow authorship wouldn't really flower until the 1970s. Then, consciousness-raising novels encouraged women to speak the truths of their lives as women, despite societal restrictions. Radical feminist novelists like Marge Piercy, Marilyn French, and Alice Walker would unite domestic themes with wide-reaching critiques of middle-class life. Women readers in the 1970s were much more comfortable with the kind of pointed political critiques that put off interwar middlebrow readers. Though Josephine Herbst insisted that "a good reader is as important in the long run as a good writer," she wouldn't find the readers it needed until the arrival of second wave feminism.

Afterword

Consequences and Transformations

The interwar convergence of women's novels, middlebrow authorship, and progressivism reached the peak of its influence during the period of the Popular Front. Much has been written about this larger cultural shift to the left in the late 1930s, notably Michael Denning's *The Cultural Front,* a massive study of cartoons, musicals, photography, theater, poetry, and fiction. The Popular Front was marked by a commitment to social justice, opposition to fascism, and "discovery" of a left-leaning American history. Fascist or imperialist advances in Germany, Italy, Japan, and Spain led radicals to seek allies in the fight against authoritarianism.

Middlebrow authors were crucial participants in the coalition of liberals, socialists, and Communists who made up the Popular Front. Scholars like Denning, for all their brilliance, tend to leave out the middle-class progressives who made the movement possible—not just FDR and the Democrats, but figures like Archibald MacLeish, Pearl Buck, and Dorothy Canfield. Without these formerly hated "liberals," no Popular Front would have been possible.

Indeed, the progressive America that writers like Canfield, Fauset, Buck, and Herbst had created became a touchstone for Popular Front mythology. Radicals moved closer to middlebrow progressives. Vernon Parrington and F. O. Matthiessen read American literature through its democratic impulses; John and Mary Beard's economic history and Van Wyck Brooks's celebrated histories of New England established a liberal political and historical tradition. In folklore and ethnography, Constance Rourke examined uniquely American traditions, especially in her most famous book, the 1934 *American Humor.* The academic disciplines of American studies and American literature grew out of these liberalizing tendencies to tell the real story of "the people."

The New Deal assisted in this embrace of American culture by claiming it as a national treasure. Through its oral history project, it preserved and funded numerous explorations of American culture, including, perhaps most famously, the autobiographies of freed slaves. The Popular Front inspired a new discovery of America, an America that could lay claim to its own unique culture, derived from the folk and unbelievably rich in its diversity. Of course, writers like Dorothy Canfield, Pearl Buck, and Jessie Fauset had been arguing for the importance of American culture and American democracy for a long time, but by the late thirties, increasing numbers of people appeared actually to agree with their views. In the late thirties, left-leaning intellectuals from liberals to Communists were claiming all of American history, folklore, and mythology as their own.

This rediscovery of American culture challenged more traditional definitions of culture, especially print culture. The preference for cultural egalitarianianism, however, made pragmatist aesthetics more respectable in literary circles than ever before; exclusive definitions of literature were an inauthentic expression of American culture. The work of librarians and educators to increase literacy and accessibility, which Dorothy Canfield had promoted in her 1927 *Why Stop Learning?,* continued in the thirties with increased governmental and public support. William Gray, in the 1935 *What Makes a Book Readable,* and Douglas Waples, in the 1938 *People and Print: Social Aspects of Reading in the Depression* and the 1940 *What Reading Does to People,* detailed the requirements of a truly national, accessible print culture and the positive benefits of such a culture. Though these studies focused on nonfiction, their emphasis on literacy contributed to a larger culture of letters on which middlebrow fiction depended.

This renewed interest in fiction's transformative power may be seen in the critical revival of nineteenth-century reform and the protest novel. By the end of the thirties, the protest novel had become a positive, distinctively American tradition, and its values in literature were no longer dismissed as hysterical dogma but passionate political sympathy. *Uncle*

Tom's Cabin became a touchstone American novel of protest, and terms that had once been used pejoratively—pity, anger, sentiment, compassion, humanity, even propaganda—were now used descriptively, even with respect and praise. It is not that reviewers and critics abandoned the more highbrow modernist aesthetics, but that they respected the intentions and rhetorical strategies of politically inflected protest novels as a tradition to be evaluated on its own terms.

By 1939, politically inflected literary criticism had become the norm in reviews, and novels in the liberal tradition were receiving increasing attention. Social protest, if not seen as the highest form of Art, at least possessed its own standards and value. Other male writers were embracing the same tradition; Ernest Hemingway's *For Whom the Bell Tolls* and Richard Wright's *Native Son* would be published the following year and chosen as Book-of-the-Month Club selections; Dorothy Canfield was a key ally in choosing Wright as the first African American selection of the BOMC.[1] Political and economic questions were paramount, and were debated fiercely in novels, in literary criticism, and in public policy.

Women writers, including those featured in this study, had been perfecting this mode of middlebrow authorship since the early twenties. Dorothy Canfield's 1939 *Seasoned Timber* is an extended fictional argument against fascism (and its accompanying anti-Semitism), and she resolves the conflict by invoking American traditions of tolerance, democracy, consensus, and antimaterialism; Pearl Buck in 1939 published *The Patriot,* a story of a Chinese man who marries in Japan and then gives up his scholarly ambivalence to fight for China against Japanese imperialism; Josephine Herbst completed her proletarian trilogy with *Rope of Gold* in 1939, which dealt with the struggle against capital and materialism in the United States and in Cuba. Only Jessie Fauset, embittered in an unhappy marriage, didn't reemerge to take advantage of the new appreciation for progressive causes and for writing that challenged the emerging modernist aesthetic. Malcolm Cowley, the noted apologist for the rootless moderns, reflects the extent of the shift in literary values. In his review of *The Patriot,* he asserts that this novel, and not the culminating novel of modern ambivalence *A House Divided,* should have completed the Wang Lung *House of Earth* trilogy, since the proper position of the modern intellectuals is not frozen indecision but brave action in battle ("Wang Lung's Children" 25). Intellectualism and practical action had merged, however briefly, in the critical consciousness.[2]

The liberal political atmosphere of 1939 and 1940, with its emphasis on democracy and freedom, recognized and celebrated a remarkable array of politically inflected texts. The Popular Front was, in many ways, the fulfillment of the coalition of middlebrow authorship, progressivism, and women's novels, a convergence of writers who sought to expand their influence on the national conscience, to establish social justice, and to evoke sympathy for cultural outsiders.

In the Popular Front, this coalition received, belatedly, a manifesto. Louise Rosenblatt, a literature professor who was deeply influenced by American pragmatism, especially by John Dewey, published *Literature as Exploration* in 1938. An often unacknowledged propounder of reader-response theory, Rosenblatt was also, I want to argue, a philosopher of the middlebrow literary experience.[3]

Rosenblatt emphasizes the triad of reader, writer, and text, and focuses on the reader's emotional reaction to a text, which creates a unique experience. She insists on the sociopolitical context of literature, and investigates the real-world consequences of reading. Though her primary focus is on the reading experience and not on authorship per se, Rosenblatt provides an idealized version of the reader, eager, engaged in making meaning, and willing to transform her life in response to the right text. This is the reader imagined in symbiotic relationship with the middlebrow writer. Rosenblatt also emphasizes the political efficacy of good reading; empowered readers, she argues, are the foundation of democracy and a functioning community. "Through literature," she writes, "the individual may develop the habit of sensing the subtle interactions of temperament upon temperament; he may come to understand the needs and aspirations of others; and he may thus make more successful adjustments in his daily relations with them" (218). She further traces the cumulative effect of individual readers of the larger society:

> This increased ability to imagine the human implications of any situation is equally important for the individual in his broader political and social relationships. Many of our greatest political blunders or social injustices are the result not so much of maliciousness or conscious cruelty as of the inability of our citizens to translate into human terms the laws or political platforms they support. . . . A democratic society, whose institutions and political and economic procedures are constantly being developed or remolded, needs citi-

> zens who will possess the social sensitivity and imagination to see what political doctrines mean for human beings. (218)

The ability to identify with others is a central tenet of middlebrow reading and writing; Rosenblatt argues it is not self-indulgent "personalism" but the foundation of a functioning democracy.

Following her own theory, Rosenblatt applies her analysis to the dire political circumstances of the late 1930s. Empowered, sympathetic readers, she argues in classic Popular Front mode, are the best defense against fascism:

> It has been said that if our imaginations functioned actively, nowhere in the world would there be a child who was starving. We should vicariously participate in his suffering—with the result that we should probably do something practical to alleviate it. . . . The way the youth in fascist countries has lent itself to a philosophy of force and brutal sadism is ample proof of the great social dangers inherent in that kind of disillusioned cynicism and flight from altruistic feeling.
>
> Lack of such imaginative sympathy is probably back of many of our present-day muddles. . . . The basis of any ultimate decision should be its meaning for actual human lives. This requires not only that we be able to understand the possible effect of our point of view upon ourselves and upon the human beings with whom we feel the kinship of family, class, or race—it is easy enough to feel these "human implications" with great intensity. We must also develop the capacity to feel intensely the needs and sufferings and aspirations of people whose personal interests are distinct from our own, people with whom we may have no bond other than our common humanity. (218–219)

Rosenblatt's theory of reading evokes the authorial constructions of Canfield, Fauset, Buck, and Herbst—emotional, deeply sympathetic, humanistic, and liberatory. The creation of such a literary conscience may lead to a world in which no child starves; the lack of it creates the brutality of Nazi Germany and Fascist Italy. No clearer connection between the emotional sympathy of women's novels and middlebrow authorship and progressive politics could be made.

Whatever "progress" society has made, Rosenblatt continues, "has been fundamentally the result of a certain extension of this kind of imagination" (219). Her claims for the transformative power of literature are measured, nevertheless bold; while it "would be absurd to suggest that literature was the cause of this . . . literature undoubtedly contributes to the diffusion of more humane sentiment" (221). She concludes:

> The ability to enter vicariously into the experience of others can be fostered by a great many different kinds of literary works. Since, as we suggested earlier, much in our individualistic society tends to make people callous to the needs of others, we should exploit this capacity of literature to nourish the imaginative flexibility that is essential to really social beings. (221)

The triad of reader, writer, and text is thus crucial to a just and free society. Rosenblatt builds on Deweyan pragmatist aesthetics to articulate the relationship between the idealized reader and writer that is so central to middlebrow authorship.

Louise Rosenblatt's work was largely forgotten in the political backlash of the 1950s, with one notable exception: in K–12 educational theory. Her emphasis on personal connections and the real-world consequences of reading have inspired progressive educators since 1938 and have become a cornerstone of literary instruction in secondary schools. This trip underground, as it were, for middlebrow writers explains the subsequent literary reputations of the writers in my study. Writers who didn't go out of print entirely, like Herbst and Fauset, were absorbed into the genre of adolescent literature; Canfield and Buck became K–12 staples. It is no accident, I want to suggest, that so many middlebrow writers were labeled as "children's writers"; Progressive education is one transmutation of middlebrow authorship, progressivism, and women's novels in the late twentieth century.

A more common narrative is not the continuation of this tradition, but its demise. The demise of the Popular Front and its vilification by McCarthyism is an oft-told tale. Dismissing middlebrow culture was a minor chord of this larger theme, as Joan Shelley Rubin points out in *The Making of Middlebrow Culture*. Clement Greenberg, Dwight Macdonald, and Robert Warshow were leading figures in a larger cultural dismissal of the middlebrow.

During the 1930s, Warshow argues, "the whole level of thought and discussion, the level of culture itself, had been lowered. . . . The mass culture of the educated classes—the culture of the 'middle-brow,' as it has sometimes been called—had come into existence" (34). The cause, he contends, was the hegemony of the Communist Party over intellectual and artistic endeavor. Thirties' radicalism, or more specifically Stalinism, "was specifically an experience of the middle class" and was "driven by . . . the insecurities of the middle class in general" (44). Because this middle class is afraid, insecure, and lazy, it seeks mass culture as an escape from real emotion and real experience; "mass culture," Warshow claims, "is the screen through which we see reality and the mirror in which we see ourselves. Its ultimate tendency is even to supersede reality" (39). True art tries to create "a valid emotional and moral response to modern life" (41), but the thirties produced prefab sentiment and clichés in its place. The acceptance both of "the pretensions of 'proletarian literature' " (36) and of *The Grapes of Wrath* as "serious literature" (35) are the legacy of the muddled thinking of the thirties' middle class.

Warshow's attack on the Popular Front comes from precisely the opposite direction as McCarthy's assault. Joe McCarthy attacked radicalism as un-American; Warshow finds the middlebrow *too* American. Echoing the assumptions of modernist authorship, which were being made canonical by the New Critics, Warshow argues that true art, by definition, struggled against the mainstream banalities of American (mass) culture. He reads even the quest for a popular, universal artistic medium as doomed, unrealistic, one that will lead only to inauthentic drivel. Writers' quest for a fictional medium to bridge economic, racial, and sexual boundaries suffered a devastating intellectual blow in the aftermath of World War II, when modernism and New Criticism fused into an academic field, an intellectual calling, and a moral good.

Clement Greenberg attacked middlebrow culture for its miscegenation. He claims that "middlebrow culture attacks distinctions as such and insinuates itself everywhere, devaluating the precious, infecting the healthy, corrupting the honest, and stultifying the wise" (879). Middlebrow blurs boundaries and confuses standards for true art. It cross-dresses as highbrow. Any writing that orients itself as both mainstream and serious, Greenberg believed, is cultural napalm.

In his germinal 1960 essay "Masscult and Midcult," Dwight Macdonald defined middlebrow culture as intellectual slumming with devastating consequences for the sedentary mind, all the more so because one may mistakenly believe it rigorous. "The tepid ooze of Midcult," he warns, "is spreading everywhere" (54), and it must be resisted because middlebrow "pretends to respect the standards of High Culture while in fact it waters them down and vulgarizes them" (37). The danger of mass culture (and its stepsister, midcult or middlebrow) is its accommodation of the needs and desires of the masses. "A mass society," he argues, "is inchoate and uncreative. . . . Its morality sinks to the level of the most primitive members . . . and its taste to that of the least sensitive and most ignorant" (9). Middlebrow authors' kinship with their readers, their willingness to entertain as well as educate, constitutes sinking to the lowest common denominator. Macdonald embraces modernist authorship's suspicion of the "common reader."

Nor is he sympathetic to middlebrow authorship's desire to heal societal divisions and construct a common American idiom. "Two cultures have developed in this country," he proclaims, "and . . . it is to the national interest to keep them separate" (72). Macdonald's conclusions represent the antithesis of Canfield, Fauset, Buck, and Herbst's quest for a democratic culture:

> The conservatives are right when they say there has never been a broadly democratic culture on a high level. This is not because the ruling class forcibly excluded the masses—this is Marxist melodrama—but quite simply because the great majority of people at any given time (including most of the ruling class for the matter) have never cared enough about such things to make them an important part of their lives. So let the masses have their Masscult, let the few who care about good writing, painting, music, architecture, philosophy, etc., have their High Culture, and don't fuzz up the distinction with Midcult. (72–73)

Dewey's "great community" gives way to an aristocracy of taste, one in which "appreciation" depends upon the scarcity of audience. Macdonald feels no responsibility to the masses. Middlebrow writers, "damnably American" (59) in Macdonald's lexicon, desire a broad audience; they are, in his estimation, more dangerous than mass culture, for middlebrow writers blur carefully constructed boundaries between life and art, high and low. In Macdonald's assumptions, one finds the key to contemporary critical dismissal of middlebrow writers.

Despite this well-known dismissal, however, the coalition of middlebrow authorship, progressivism, and women's novels has kept reemerging in American literary culture, under other guises. In seventies' consciousness-raising novels and Oprah's Book Club, it has continued to influence contemporary literary culture.

Second wave feminism was a political movement with deep roots in the radical social activism of the 1960s. It was also a movement that made the telling of stories central. Reading the manifestations of culture personally and passionately was the fundamental gesture of the movement, the impetus behind the slogan "the personal is the political." Second wave feminism used reading and writing to build the women's community; consciousness-raising novels, in Gayle Greene's analysis, "transformed confusion to consciousness, enabling women to understand the changes they were living through" (50). Women readers were encouraged to universalize their own and other women's experience (Hogeland xiii), to identify with stories and apply them to their own lives. Consciousness-raising novelists eschewed modernist experimentation for more familiar realist narrative strategies that focus on the novel as a social investigation (Greene 5), and they wanted a large readership of women, not a small, educated core (3). Popular novelists like Erica Jong, Marge Piercy, Marilyn French, and Alice Walker brought feminist ideals to middle-class women readers (Hogeland ix–x). These writers could further connect with their readers through *Ms.* Magazine, founded by Gloria Steinem. *Ms.* created a progressive alternative to traditional women's magazines while still drawing on that readership; Amy Farrell calls this combination a "bold experiment" to resolve the reformist/ revolutionary split of second wave feminism (14).

This brand of "cultural feminism" has been thoroughly critiqued for being accommodationist, middle-class, white-identified, and inadequately racial—in a word, for being middlebrow. Popular consciousness-raising novels extended a mode of authorship exemplified by Canfield, Buck, Fauset, and Herbst. These popular feminist novelists tended to cite nineteenth-century forebears because they were, by and large, unaware of their interwar foremothers. But their approaches, formal choices, and focus on the experience of the reader connect them with this forgotten tradition of authorship.

The most recent manifestation of this mode of authorship has come through Oprah's Book Club—geared toward women, focused on the personal experience of reading, and vilified by "serious" novelists in similar ways. Cecilia Farr argues that Oprah's Book Club has a middlebrow aesthetic and focuses on women's personal experience to encourage a broader cultural democracy (145). Oprah's Book Club, of course, has been as controversial in its day as the Book-of-the-Month Club was in the twenties, with grateful publishers and also doomsday critics predicting the end of American letters. Jonathan Franzen's public break with the Book Club, his suspicion of its commercialism and his reluctance to be categorized as a women's novelist, show how relevant debates on gender, middlebrow, and authorship continue to be. Change "Oprah's Book Club" to "the Book-of-the-Month Club," "Oprah Winfrey" to "Dorothy Canfield," and this debate evokes the antimiddlebrow rhetoric of the twenties.

There are of course, significant differences between the middlebrow culture of the interwar period and Oprah's Book Club. Books are selected based on Oprah's personal magnetism and her love of a book, which she insists her viewers must also love. And while interwar writers like Canfield were criticized for being overly conventional—for choosing self-sacrifice over self-realization—Oprah's Book Club writers are seen as simply another version of The Oprah Show's relentless therapeutic navel-gazing. In both cases however, the "apolitical personalism" of middlebrow writers is a key issue.

Oprah's Book Club writers, of course, are a diverse group. Many of the books, like Barbara Kingsolver's *Poisonwood Bible,* offer substantial critiques of American foreign policy, cultural chauvinism, and religious intolerance. Others, like Toni Morrison's *Song of Solomon* and *Paradise,* not only assail American racism, but also provide nuanced investigations of political movements and their ramifications. When readers relate these books to their own lives on the show, they often bypass the political nuances. Oprah's continued emphasis on the transformative power of books, however, shows the same faith in readers' ability to learn and changes that fueled the writing of the authors examined in this study.

We have yet to develop the critical tools to recognize this kind of writing as a legitimate mode of authorship, as Tad Friend argued in 1992. "We have lost appreciation," he claims, "for the art that was once the mainstay of American culture and the unguilty delight of intelligent readers, listeners, and viewers: the art of the middlebrow" (24). Middlebrow writing, exemplified by Harriet Beecher Stowe's *Uncle Tom's Cabin* and Upton Sinclair's *The Jungle,* is "unmediated," "direct," and "never, ever hip";

it "is distinguished by technical competence, singleness of affect, purity of emotion, tidiness of resolution, and modesty of scope" (25). Middlebrow texts seek to unite emotion and intellect (they want the reader to "feel and think at the same time" [27]) and unfashionably believe in "our common humanity." Friend advocates skillful middlebrow writing, which "further[s] the notion that art, all art, should disclose not secrets to the few, but treasures to the many" (27). *America the Middlebrow* has excavated part of the genealogy of women's novels, progressivism, and middlebrow authorship. Interwar women writers exhibited a passionate devotion to America's possibilities, and reshaped American iconography toward progressive ends. Serious investigation of the equivocations, failures, and triumphs of these writers may broaden American literary criticism.

Notes

INTRODUCTION

1. See Jane Tompkins, *Sensational Designs;* Nina Baym, *Woman's Fiction;* Joan Hedrick, *Harriet Beecher Stowe;* Carolyn Karcher, *First Woman of the Republic;* Judith Fetterley, *The Resisting Reader;* Amy Kaplan, *The Social Construction of American Realism;* Mary Kelley, *Private Woman, Public Stage.*

2. See Richard Hofstadter, *The Age of Reform;* Gabriel Kolko, *The Triumph of Conservatism;* James Weinstein, *The Corporate Ideal in the Liberal State;* Warren Susman, *Culture as History;* and Martin Sklar, *The Corporate Reconstruction of American Capitalism.*

3. George Hutchinson, in *The Harlem Renaissance in Black and White,* traces the influence of pragmatist aesthetics on Harlem Renaissance writers and critics, particularly Alain Locke. My argument regarding pragmatist aesthetics is deeply indebted to Hutchinson's work.

4. For a more detailed investigation of Progressive women writers, see Carol J. Batker's *Reforming Fictions.*

5. See Lisa Botshon and Meredith Goldsmith's *Middlebrow Moderns: American Women Writers of the 1920s;* Deborah Lindsay Williams's *Not in Sisterhood;* and Julia Ehrhardt's *Writers of Conviction.*

6. Kevin J. H. Dettmar and Stephen Watt, eds., *Marketing Modernisms;* Jani Scadura and Michael Thurston, eds., *Modernism, Inc.;* Jay Satterfield, "*The World's Best Books": Taste, Culture, and the Modern Library;* Mark Morrisson, *The Public Face of Modernism;* Catherine Turner, *Marketing Modernism between the Two World Wars.*

7. Frederic Jameson, "Beyond the Cave: Demystifying the Ideology of Modernism"; Paul Morrison, *The Poetics of Fascism.*

8. A selected list of studies of authorship includes William Charvat's *Literary Publishing in America 1790–1850;* James West's *American Authors and the Literary Marketplace since 1900,* Christopher Wilson's *The Labor of Words;* and Susan Coultrap-McQuin's *Doing Literary Business.*

9. Joan Shelley Rubin's 1992 *The Making of Middlebrow Culture* initiated critical attention to middlebrow culture in the first half of the twentieth century; Janice Radway's 1997 *A Feeling for Books: The Book-of-the-Month Club, Literary Taste, and Middle-Class Desire* further stimulated academic interest. Recent studies include investigations of British middlebrow culture, of popular American women writers of the 1920s, and of the creation of "middle" America. See Nicola Humble, *The Feminine Middlebrow Novel, 1920s to 1950s;* Lisa Botshon and Meredith Goldsmith, *Middlebrow Moderns;* and Jennifer Parchesky, *Melodramas of Everyday Life.*

10. See Gordon Hutner's essay "In the Middle: Fiction, Borders, and Class."

CHAPTER ONE

1. Cather, forced to replace the story, added "Flavia and her Artists," a devastating satire on a horribly superficial artiste and her long-suffering husband. "Flavia" was Canfield's mother's name, and the story's marital portrait closely suggests Canfield's own parents, whom Cather had had ample time to observe when James Hulme Canfield was the president of the University of Nebraska. Cather thus got the last word, but she also got fifteen years of estrangement. She and Canfield were not reconciled until after James Hulme Canfield's death.

2. Malcolm Cowley, the early chronicler of modernism in books like *Exile's Return,* invoked her to dismiss the New Humanists; in 1929, the year of *The Sound and the Fury, A Farewell to Arms,* and *Look Homeward, Angel,* he wrote that "the academic Humanists bring out a symposium proving, among other things, that there are no good American writers except maybe Dorothy Canfield" (*After the Genteel Tradition* 196). Mark Madigan argues that her "authentic narratives of everyday American life were deemed unfashionable, her narrative technique was considered too conventional, and she was relegated to a marginal position in the literary pantheon" (6).

3. For example, Canfield published her own response to the anti-immigrant hysteria of "middle America" in a short story in the muckraking *Everybody's Magazine.* An outsider visits a New England town in decay. A young woman, saddled with the care of her invalid mother, is forced into the role of New England spinster, living in a town with no economy and no discernible future, and the visitor bemoans her fate. On returning to the town years later, however, she finds her married and thriving. How was this traditional local-color story transformed? The young woman aids an Italian immigrant in his escape from indenture and marries him, and he adapts her barren farmland to the production of goat cheese for other Italians in the city. The story ends with a *My Antonia*–like image of fecundity as the family comes home from work in the pasture.

4. Bok's attitude has often been seen as the approach of all women's magazines. Helen Damon-Moore, in her study of *The Ladies' Home Journal,* characterizes the common male editor's attitude toward women readers as condescending. She cites Betty Friedan's report of a response from a woman's-magazine editor as typical: "Our readers are housewives, full time. They're not interested in national or international affairs. They are only interested in the family and the home. They aren't interested in politics, unless it's related to an immediate need in the home, like the price of coffee. . . . You just can't write about ideas or broad issues of the day for women" (Damon-Moore 197).

5. Canfield's balanced "presentation" of racial conflict, for example, or class conflict, was often far too forgiving of her audience's prejudices. In her letters, she gently upbraided Pearl S. Buck for too insistently demanding immediate rectification of racism (Letter to Buck 27 August 1943). Jennifer Parchesky has noted her frequent pathologizing of the lower class, especially in *Her Son's Wife* (1926) and *Bonfire* (1933); its filth and laziness, she implies, are responsible for shabby treatment of women and profound character lapses. And Julia Ehrhardt's elaboration of the interest in eugenics embedded in her fetish for genealogy, heritage, and the ethnic purity of Vermont demonstrates persuasively that despite her often courageous advocacy for African Americans, Canfield's views on ethnic diversity were not nearly as enlightened as one would hope.

CHAPTER TWO

1. Susan Tomlinson and Deborah Chay have reviewed the negative criticism that affected Fauset's reputation. See Chay, *Black Feminist Criticism and the Politics of Reading Jessie Fauset,* and Tomlinson, *Changing Meanings of Jessie Fauset.*

2. Their relationship wasmore than professional. Du Bois biographer David Levering Lewis identifies Fauset as one of Du Bois's many extramarital affairs (*W. E. B. Du Bois: Biography of a Race* 464). Fauset seems to have harbored illusions of becoming the second Mrs. Du Bois, and waited over twenty years for the opportunity, before marrying a New Jersey businessman at the age of forty-seven. DuBois's intellectual and artistic influence on Fauset was immense. When their personal, and then their professional, relationship deteriorated in 1926 (Lewis *W. E. B. Du Bois: The Fight For Equality* 189–190), Du Bois turned away from literature (180–181), and Fauset's professional ambitions also foundered.

3. Unlike the other writers in this study, Fauset did not donate her papers to a library, nor did her two publishers, Boni & Liveright and Frederick A. Stokes; both were acquired by other presses, which were then bought again. Her literary agency, Brandt & Brandt (now Brandt and Hochman), has a record of contracts, sales, and royalties, but no correspondence. Most information about her experience with publishers and agents has come from her letters to Harlem Renaissance writers Countee Cullen and Langston Hughes. Because of this lack of information, my discussion of Fauset's publishing experience is necessarily speculative rather than definitive.

CHAPTER THREE

1. This explains why she found Faulkner, in particular, so puzzling. When she was trying to (re)acquaint herself with America, she asked Richard Walsh to recommend the most talented American writers, and he mentioned William Faulkner. Buck found *Sanctuary* and *Light in August* incomprehensible. "I feel wholly discouraged about myself," she wrote to Walsh,

> for, although I read them word for word in order to try to understand them, I do not know what they say. Such life is expressed in terms I cannot comprehend—I do not know that life nor have those persons any meaning for me. I am discouraged because if he is one of the best and most promising American writers, then I can never write about Americans, after all. I do not mean I do not admire his writing—I do like it very much—the sheer writing—but I cannot feel reality anywhere—I do not know what he means. (Letter to Walsh 7 November 1932)

At first glance, an unsympathetic reader might assume that Buck wasn't smart enough to understand Faulkner; a closer reading shows a more interesting clash of literary values. Buck admires "the sheer writing," but it doesn't let her "feel reality"—to comprehend the South's complexity and tragedy. Buck's failure is even more interesting since her parents were Southern and she went to college in the South; she should have had some knowledge to bring to reading Faulkner. And yet, the "life" of the story "is expressed in terms [she] cannot comprehend." One can only speculate about which features of Faulkner's writing alienated her—his long, complex sentences, shifting perspectives, nonlinear narratives, or perhaps his fatalism in the face of racial guilt.

Faulkner, of course, saw his own authorship in dramatically different terms—a writer underappreciated in his own time, writing not for the people with whom he had grown up and continued to live but for some future, cultured audience; a writer who wrote with clarity about social ills and injustice, but who rejected any practical attempt to remedy those injustices. No two Nobel Prize winners could have had more opposing notions of authorship.

Of course, Buck didn't come to her aesthetic with the confidence that American modernists had. While she could appreciate Faulkner despite being mystified by his authorial assumptions, he could view her only with disdain, calling her "Old China Hand Buck" (Blotner 1342). Buck had a broader view of literary aesthetic and literary merit than did the American modernists.

2. Walsh, Transcript of radio broadcast, 1932.

3. Malcolm Cowley, in his critique of his generation's unrootedness, discusses their summer homes in Connecticut as a kind of sin against the land, because they were nomads, not tillers. Quoting from a Robert Coates novel, Cowley wonders if there is a "law concerning the rights of the soil to expect careful husbandry on the part of its owner" (*Exile's Return* 210). He continues: "Perhaps such a law exists,

though still unwritten; perhaps it levies its quiet penalties against the man that holds even stony acres without plowing them, or lives in a community without taking part in its life" (210–211).

CHAPTER FOUR

1. Herbst's papers were preserved because of her connections with the famous and her first editions, and because of her desire that they be preserved; Yale wasn't particularly interested in her as a writer, but they were very interested in who she knew and what she had collected (Langer 327).

2. Of course, the very definition of the "proletarian novel" was anything but settled, least of all, as Barbara Foley indicates, by proletarian practitioners themselves. Was a "proletarian novel" one written *by* a "proletarian" or *for* a "proletarian"? Did a "proletarian novel" allow only certain subjects and themes? (For many critics in the thirties, "proletarian novel" was synonymous with "strike novel," because of the preponderance of strikes in proletarian novels. One incident, the 1929 Gastonia strike in North Carolina, inspired six different novels.) Does a "proletarian novel" require explicit class consciousness on the part of workers, or a conversion experience, like the famous ending of Mike Gold's 1929 *Jews without Money?* Many writers, especially those who were characterized by the label, debated the validity of the term at all, among them Josephine Herbst, John Steinbeck, and James T. Farrell, creator of the famous *Studs Lonigan* series. Despite its slipperiness, however, the label "proletarian" did indicate unifying attitudes and intentions, if it couldn't predict form or theme.

3. See Robert McElvaine, *The Great Depression,* and Michael Denning, *The Cultural Front.*

4. In a July 1934 series of articles critiquing the anticommunism of John Dewey, Bertrand Russell, and Morris Cohen, the *New Masses* alleged that their rejection of revolution "perpetuate[s] a system whose essence means incessant misery for the masses of mankind, incessant starvation, torture, degradation"; their "liberalism," Paul Salter and Jack Librome concluded, "is a deep-rooted fear of wide social change." In a May 1934 review of Harold Stearns's *Rediscovering America,* Bernard Smith took the opportunity to write another *New Masses* eulogy for liberalism (this one entitled "Another Liberal Collapses"). "It is hardly necessary today," proclaimed Smith with admirable confidence, "to expand the subject of liberalism's failure"; all that is left is nostalgic respect for liberals like Stearns, "a symbol of the last valiant struggle of liberalism—an attractive and irreproachable figure personifying an era now fortunately done with" (15 May 1934).

5. The introduction to this advice column, titled "Cupid's Letter Box," is saturated with irony: "Liberals and progressives, are you unhappy? Do grown-ups refuse to sympathize, and even make fun of your heart's desire? Of course! Then tell your troubles to Cupid—*he* will understand" (Smith 30). After this promising beginning, Cupid dispenses tongue-in-cheek advice, such as this, to the philandering priest: "Father quit pretending. You're a natural born lout and you know it."

6. Herbst critiques a larger conservative trend in the thirties. For example, in 1930, as part of the short-lived New Humanist movement (which even the *Saturday Review* termed fascist), Irving Babbitt outraged liberals and radicals when he claimed that the rights of property were more sacred than the rights of individuals.

7. Reader reports, the initial review process that decided which books went to the five judges, were not preserved for *The Executioner Waits* (nor were any BOMC records until 1939), but luckily the initial reader reports for her next novel, *Rope of Gold,* do exist, and they provide a useful commentary on how an imaginary "general reader" might react to her formal choices.

AFTERWORD

1. Dorothy Canfield, long a champion of both causes, lobbied for the selection of *Native Son* and served as an informal mentor to Wright in his continued attempts to reach an American mainstream audience. The selection of *Native Son* suggests progressive middlebrow authorship's larger cultural significance as a key ally for radical movements that expand the possibilities of American public discourse.

Before *Native Son,* the Book-of-the-Month Club had not selected a novel by an African American as its primary book of the month. Such an omission is striking given the liberalism of the board of judges, and especially considering Canfield's outspoken advocacy of civil rights. Because the Book-of-the-Month Club preserved no records before 1939, it is impossible to state with certainty the reasons for it. Fear, unwillingness to offend, and a restrictive sense of what "general readers" could stand doubtless played a part. The initial reader reports of the novel reveal much about why *Native Son* was the first African American novel the BOMC chose. One reader wrote that "the subject will preclude" *Native Son's* selection, but requested a second opinion because "it has a quality that cannot be escaped, and because I reacted to it so strongly that I find myself unable to look through it again to verify first impressions" (Reader Report *Native Son*). The book was powerful, even though the emotions it depicted were "horror, fear, and hate." The second reader had an even more difficult time reading the novel, but felt transformed by the experience:

> This novel is very horrible and at the same time very moving. I had difficulty reading it, not because I was indifferent but because it made me so uncomfortable and so unhappy. . . . I think the judges should consider it for the recommended list, for it is honest, profoundly shocking to aryan complacency, and dramatically told. (Reader Report *Native Son*)

Again, what swayed the readers, despite the novel's aggressive indictment of white racism, was *its* emotional power. It made its readers sympathize with the experience of a black rapist and murderer, a figure James Baldwin later identifies as the bogey of white American consciousness. *Native Son* was also uniquely attuned to the emotional, identificatory quality of middlebrow reading.

Harry Scherman, in an unusual move for him, wrote his own reader's report to bring the novel to the attention of Dorothy Canfield and the rest of the board. The book, he wrote "is a powerful indictment," which "must not be dismissed as a propaganda novel. The author is a negro communist and there is propaganda in it. But the emotion is far deeper than any idea could foster" (Reader Report *Native Son*). Praising its emotionally transformative power, its "comprehension" and "inspiration," Scherman called *Native Son* "a sort of 1939 Uncle Tom's Cabin," and concluded, "I don't know how much the public can take, but I think this should be read as an A book." For Scherman, then, and ultimately for the BOMC board, *Native Son* was intelligiblewithin the American protest tradition, and as such it could influence a broad audience.

2. The interpretive community of the Popular Front drew in even writers whose aesthetic and political proclivities were at odds with liberalism. Willa Cather's 1940 *Sapphira and the Slave Girl* is a case in point. The novel is a strange one in the career of Cather, who had always been hostile to liberal activism and, during the New Deal, had become anti-Roosevelt. *Sapphira* employs very strange, even offensive, racial dynamics, incorporating an oral sex scene, and in the end seems to embrace the authoritarian, hierarchical Sapphira, not the escaped slave Nancy, as its hero. And yet, in its Book-of-the-Month Club introduction, written by Dorothy Canfield, the novel appears to be a modern liberatory slave narrative. As Canfield wrote in the *Book of the Month Club News,*

> The people of our times are turned towards embittered skepticism by calamity almost beyond human imagining. Helpless spectators of the horrifying spread of human slavery, readers of 1940 are forced into a suspicion that a happy ending to any story can be no more than a cheap and sleazy veil thrown over but not hiding the ugly figure of truth. To such saddened readers, aching with shame for humanity, Willa Cather presents a lovely story of escape from human slavery, which is not only literally and factually true, but deeply and symbolically true. . . . Those values are infinitely consoling and comforting to us, shocked as we are by the recurring, ever-nearer dangers to our own freedom. This book bids us have faith. ("Sapphira and the Slave Girl" 2–3)

Cather may have wanted to write outside of the political, but her book could not help but speak to thecrisis so many felt in 1940; Canfield transforms the novel into a fable for the struggle against fascism.

3. For more information on Louise Rosenblatt and her legacy, see Clifford, *The Experience of Reading.*

Works Cited

Adamic, Louis. "What the Proletariat Reads: Conclusions Based on a Year's Study among Hundreds of Workers throughout the United States." *Saturday Review of Literature* 11.20 (1 December 1934): 321–322.

Adorno, Theodor. "On Commitment." In *The Essential Frankfurt School Reader*, ed. Andrew Arato and Eike Gebhardt. New York: Urizen, 1978.

Advertisement for *All Men Are Brothers*. John Day Publishers, Pearl Buck Collection, Princeton University Library.

Advertisement for *There Is Confusion*. *New York Times Book Review* 13 April 1924.

Batker, Carol J. *Reforming Fictions: Native, African, and Jewish American Women's Literature and Journalism in the Progressive Era*. New York: Columbia University Press, 2000.

Baym, Nina. *Woman's Fiction: A Guide to Novels by and About Women in America, 1820–70*. 2d. ed. Urbana: University of Illinois Press, 1993.

Black, Helen. Letter to Josephine Herbst. 4 December 1928. Josephine Herbst Collection, Beinecke Library, Yale University.

Blotner, Joseph. *Faulkner: A Biography*. Vol. 2. New York: Random House, 1974.

Botshon, Lisa, and Meredith Goldsmith, eds. *Middlebrow Moderns: Popular American Women Writers of the 1920s*. Boston: Northeastern University Press, 2003.

Boynton, Percy H. "Two New England Regionalists." *College English* 1.4 (January 1940): 291–299.

Brandt and Hochman Literary Agency. Royalties card, Jessie Fauset.

Bruccoli, Matthew. *James Gould Cozzens: A Life Apart.* San Diego: Harcourt Brace Jovanovich, 1983.

Buck, Pearl. "A Note by the Translator." *All Men Are Brothers.* New York: John Day, 1933.

———. "Bestsellers." League of American Writers 29 November 1939. John Day Publishers, Pearl Buck Collection, Princeton University Library.

———. *The Chinese Novel: Nobel Lecture Delivered before the Swedish Academy at Stockholm, December 12, 1938.* New York: John Day, 1939.

———. *The Good Earth.* (1931). New York: Pocket Books, 1969.

———. "In China, Too." *Atlantic Monthly* January 1923: 68–72.

———. Letter to John Day. 22 July 1931; 22 March 1932. John Day Publishers, Pearl Buck Collection, Princeton University Library.

———. Letter to Richard Walsh. 25 June and 9 September 1930; 26 January, 25 February, 28 April, 3 June, and 30 July 1931; 23 February, 3 May, and 7 November 1932. John Day Publishers, Pearl Buck Collection, Princeton University Library.

———. *My Several Worlds, a Personal Record.* New York: John Day, 1954.

Caldwell, Erskine. Letter to Harcourt Brace. Undated. Josephine Herbst Collection, Beinecke Library, Yale University.

Canfield, Dorothy. "An American Citizen." *The Crisis* April–May, 1920.

———. *The Bedquilt and Other Stories.* Ed. Mark Madigan. Columbia: University of Missouri Press, 1996.

———. "Book Clubs." *Dorothy Canfield Fisher: In Memoriam.* New York: Book-of-the-Month Club, 1958.

———. *The Brimming Cup.* (1921) New York: Virago Press, 1987.

———. Letter to Pearl Buck. 27 August 1943. Dorothy Canfield Fisher Collection, Bailey/Howe Library, University of Vermont.

———. Letter to Alfred Harcourt. 10 November 1920; 9 and 26 October 1922. Dorothy Canfield Fisher Collection, Bailey/Howe Library, University of Vermont.

———. Letter to Paul Reynolds. 6, 9, 12, and 17 February 1920. Paul Reynolds Collection, Columbia University Library.

———. Letter to Harry Scherman. 1931. Dorothy Canfield Fisher Collection, Bailey/Howe Library, University of Vermont.

———. "Sapphira and the Slave Girl." *Book-of-the-Month Club News.* December 1940.

———. *Seasoned Timber.* New York: Harcourt, 1939.

———. *Vermont Tradition: Biography of an Outlook on Life.* Boston: Little, Brown, 1953.

———. *Why Stop Learning?* New York: Harcourt, Brace, 1927.

Charvat, William. *Literary Publishing in America, 1790–1850.* (1959) Amherst: University of Massachusetts Press, 1993.

Chay, Deborah. "Black Feminist Criticism and the Politics of Reading Jessie Fauset." Diss., Duke University, 1993.
Christian, Barbara. *Black Women Novelists: The Development of a Tradition, 1892–1976*. Westport, Conn.: Greenwood, 1980.
Clifford, John, ed. *The Experience of Reading: Louise Rosenblatt and Reader-Response Theory*. Portsmouth, N.H.: Boynton/Cook, 1990.
Conn, Peter J. *Pearl S. Buck: A Cultural Biography*. New York: Cambridge University Press, 1996.
Coultrap-McQuin, Susan. *Doing Literary Business: American Women Writers in the Nineteenth Century*. Chapel Hill:University of North Carolina Press, 1990.
Cowley, Malcolm. *After the Genteel Tradition: American Writers, 1910–1930*. (1937) Carbondale: Southern Illinois University Press, 1964.
———. *Exile's Return: A Literary Odyssey of the 1920s*. (1934) New York: Viking, 1964.
———. Introduction. *The Selected Writings of Lafcadio Hearn*, ed. Henry Goodman. New York: Citadel, 1949.
———. "Wang Lung's Children." *New Republic* 4 March 1939: 24–25.
———. "Revolutionary Movement and Writer." In *American Writers Congress*, ed. Henry Hart. New York: International Publishers, 1935.
Damon-Moore, Helen. *Magazines for the Millions: Gender and Commerce in the "Ladies' Home Journal" and the "Saturday Evening Post" 1880–1910*. Albany: State University of New York Press, 1994.
Dardis, Tom. *Firebrand: The Life of Horace Liveright*. New York: Random House, 1995.
Davis, Peggy. Letter to Dorothy Canfield. 9 July 1940. Fan Letters, Dorothy Canfield Fisher Collection, Bailey/Howe Library, University of Vermont.
Denning, Michael. *The Cultural Front: The Laboring of American Culture in the Twentieth Century*. New York: Verso, 1998.
Desbecker, Mrs. Richard W. Letter to Dorothy Canfield Fisher. 1 March 1957. Fan Letters, Dorothy Canfield Fisher Collection, Bailey/Howe Library, University of Vermont.
Dettmar, Kevin J. H. and Stephen Watt, eds. *Marketing Modernisms: Self-Promotion, Canonization, and Rereading*. Ann Arbor: University of Michigan Press, 1996.
Dewey, John. *Art as Experience*. New York: Minton, Balch, 1934.
———. *Democracy and Education: An Introduction to the Philosophy of Education*. New York: Macmillan, 1916.
———. *Liberalism and Social Action*. New York: G. P. Putnam's Sons, 1935.
Douglas, Ann. *Terrible Honesty: Mongrel Manhattan in the 1920s*. New York: Farrar, Straus and Giroux, 1995.
Du Bois, W. E . B. Letter to Jessie Fauset. 25 September 1934. W. E. B. Du Bois Collection, W. E. B. Du Bois Library, University of Massachusetts Amherst.

DuPlessis, Rachel. *The Pink Guitar: Writing as Feminist Practice.* New York: Routledge, 1990.

Ehrhardt, Julia. *Writers of Conviction: The Personal Politics of Zona Gale, Dorothy Canfield Fisher, Rose Wilder Lane, and Josephine Herbst.* Columbia: University of Missouri Press, 2004.

Evans, Nancy. Review of *The Good Earth. The Bookman* 73 (May 1931): 324.

Farr, Cecilia Konchar. *Reading Oprah: How Oprah's Book Club Changed the Way America Reads.* Albany: State University of New York Press, 2005.

Farrell, Amy. *Yours in Sisterhood: Ms. Magazine and the Promise of Popular Feminism.* Durham: University of North Carolina Press, 1998.

Fauset, Jessie Redmon. Letter to Du Bois. 16 February 1905; 27 February 1907; and 7 April 1919. W. E. B. Du Bois Collection, W. E. B. Du Bois Library, University of Massachusetts Amherst.

———. Letter to Zona Gale. 22 October 1931. Zona Gale Papers, Wisconsin Historical Society.

———. Letter to Langston Hughes. Undated; 28 May 1923; 20 April 1924; 23 September 1925; 1926; 9 June and 22 October 1949; 2 October 1950. James Weldon Johnson Collection, Langston Hughes correspondence, Beinecke Library, Yale University.

———. Letter to Georgia Douglas Johnson. 22 September 1924. Georgia Douglas Johnson Papers, Moorland-Spingarn Research Center, Howard University.

———. Letter to Alain Locke. Undated; 9 and 10 January 1933. Alain Locke Collection, Moorland-Spingarn Research Center, Howard University.

———. Letter to Jesse Moorland. Undated. Jesse Moorland Collection, Moorland-Spingarn Research Center, Howard University.

———. Letter to Joel Spingarn. 1913. Spingarn Collection, Moorland-Spingarn Research Center, Howard University.

———. Letter to Jean Toomer. 17 and 24 February 1922. James Weldon Johnson Collection, Jean Toomer, Beinecke Library, Yale University.

———. "My Home." Letter to Du Bois. 27 February 1907. W. E .B. Du Bois Collection, W. E .B. Du Bois Library, University of Massachusetts Amherst.

———. "Nostalgia." *The Crisis* 22.4 (August 1921): 154–158.

———. *Plum Bun: A Novel without a Moral.* (1929) Boston: Pandora Press, 1985.

———. "The Symbolism of Bert Williams." *The Crisis* 24.1 (May 1922): 12–15.

———. *There Is Confusion.* New York: Boni & Liveright, 1924.

———. "When Christmas Comes." *The Crisis* 28.2 (December 1922): 61–63.

Fetterley, Judith. *The Resisting Reader: A Feminist Approach to American Fiction.* (1978) Urbana: University of Illinois Press, 1981.

Foley, Barbara. *Radical Representations: Politics and Form in U.S. Proletarian Fiction, 1929–1941.* Durham, N.C.: Duke University Press, 1993.

Freeman, Joseph. "Ivory Towers—White and Red." *New Masses* 11 September 1934: 20.

Friend, Tad. "The Case for Middlebrow." *New Republic* March 1992: 24–27.

Frost, Robert. "From Robert Frost." *Dorothy Canfield Fisher: In Memoriam.* New York: Book-of-the Month Club, 1958.

Garlin, Sender. "Upton Sinclair: Reactionary Utopian." *New Masses* 18 September 1934.

Gilbert, Sandra M., and Susan Gubar. *No Man's Land: The Place of the Woman Writer in The Twentieth Century.* New Haven, Conn.: Yale University Press, 1988.

Greenberg, Clement. "State of American Writing." *Partisan Review* 15 (1948): 876–883.

Greene, Gayle. *Changing the Story: Feminist Fiction and the Tradition.* Bloomington: Indiana University Press, 1990.

Gregory, Horace. "Review of *The Executioner Waits.*" *Books* (28 October 1934): 4.

Harcourt, Alfred. Letter to Dorothy Canfield. 13 June 1933. Dorothy Canfield Fisher Collection, Bailey/Howe Library, University of Vermont.

———. *Some Experiences.* Riverside, Conn.: Privately printed by Alfred and Ellen Harcourt, 1951.

Harcourt, Brace News. "The Executioner Waits." 18 September 1934. Josephine Herbst Collection. Beinecke Library, Yale University.

Hart, Henry, ed. *American Writers Congress.* New York: International Publishers, 1935.

Hedrick, Joan. *Harriet Beecher Stowe: A Life.* New York: Oxford University Press, 1994.

Herbst, Josephine. *The Executioner Waits.* New York: Harcourt, Brace, 1934.

———. Letter to Monty Penkower. 18 December 1967. Josephine Herbst Collection, Beinecke Library, Yale University.

———. Letter to William A. Sutton. 6 February 1968. Josephine Herbst Collection, Beinecke Library, Yale University.

Hicks, Granville. "An Open Letter." *New Masses.* 2 January 1934: 24.

———. "Revolution and the Novel. I: The Past and Future as Themes." *New Masses* 3 April 1934.

———. "White Guards on Parade." *New Masses* 2 October 1934.

Hochman, Barbara. *Getting at the Author: Reimagining Books and Reading in the Age of American Realism.* Amherst: University of Massachusetts Press, 2001.

Hofstadter, Richard. *The Age of Reform: From Bryan to F.D.R.* New York: Knopf, 1955.

Hogeland, Lisa. *Feminism and Its Fictions: The Consciousness-Raising Novel and the Women's Liberation Movement.* Philadelphia: University of Pennsylvania Press, 1998.

Huff Fauset, Arthur. "Autobiography." Manuscript. Arthur Huff Fauset Collection, University of Pennsylvania.

Humble, Nicola. *The Feminine Middlebrow Novel, 1920s to 1950s: Class, Domesticity, and Bohemianism.* New York: Oxford University Press, 2001.

Hutchinson, George. *The Harlem Renaissance in Black and White.* Cambridge, Mass.: Belknap Press of Harvard University Press, 1995.

Hutchisson, James. *The Rise of Sinclair Lewis, 1920–1930.* University Park: Pennsylvania State University Press, 1996.

Hutner, Gordon. "In the Middle: Fiction, Borders, and Class." *CR: The New Centennial Review* 1.2 (Fall 2001): 89–108.

James, William. *Pragmatism: A New Name for Some Old Ways of Thinking: Popular Lectures on Philosophy.* New York: Longmans, Green, 1907.

Jameson, Frederic. "Beyond the "Cave: Demystifying the Ideology of Modernism." In *The Ideologies of Theory, Essays 1971–1986.* Minneapolis: University of Minnesota Press, 1988.

Johnson, James Weldon. "The Dilemma of the Negro Author." *American Mercury* December 1928: 477–481.

Kang, Younghill. Review of *The Good Earth. New Republic* 1 July 1931: 185.

Kaplan, Amy. *The Social Construction of American Realism.* Chicago: University of Chicago Press, 1988.

Karcher, Carolyn. *The First Woman in the Republic: A Cultural Biography of Lydia Maria Child.* Durham, N.C.: Duke University Press, 1994.

Kelley, Mary. *Private Woman, Public Stage: Literary Domesticity in Nineteenth-Century America.* (1984) Chapel Hill: University of North Carolina Press, 2002.

Kirchway, Freda. "Victory Before Battle." *The Nation* 7 December 1921: 113.

Kolko, Gabriel. *The Triumph of Conservatism.* New York: Free Press, 1963.

Kowallis, Jon Eugene von. *The Lyrical Lu Xun: A Study of His Classical-Style Verse.* Honolulu: University of Hawai'i Press, 1996.

Lamont, Corliss. "John Dewey Capitulates to 'God.' " *New Masses* 31 July 1934: 23–24.

Langer, Elinor. *Josephine Herbst.* (1984) Boston: Northeastern University Press, 1994.

Leong, Karen J. *The China Mystique: Pearl S. Buck, Anna May Wong, Mayling Soong, and the Transformation of American Orientialism.* Berkeley: University of California Press, 2005.

Le Sueur, Meridel. "The Fetish of Being Outside." (1935) In *Harvest Song: Collected Essays and Stories.* Albuquerque, N.M.: West End Press, 1990. Pp.199–203.

Lewis, David Levering. *W. E. B. Du Bois: Biography of a Race, 1868–1919.* New York: Holt, 1993.

———. *W. E. B. Du Bois: The Fight For Equality and the American Century, 1919–1963.* New York: Holt, 2000.

———. *When Harlem Was in Vogue.* New York: Vintage, 1981.

Lewis, Sinclair. Foreward. *Henry Ward Beecher: An American Portrait,* ed. Paxton Hibben. New York: Press of the Readers Club, 1942.

Liao, Kang. *Pearl S. Buck: A Cultural Bridge across the Pacific.* Westport, Conn.: Greenwood, 1997.

Lieber, Maxim. Letter to Josephine Herbst. 1 June 1931; 22 November 1932. Josephine Herbst Collection, Beinecke Library, Yale University.

Lloyd, David. Letter to Richard Walsh. 28 April 1931. John Day Collection. Princeton University Library.

———. Letter to Mr. Rimington. 25 June 1930. John Day Collection. Princeton University Library.

Locke, Alain. Letter to Jessie Fauset. Undated. Alain Locke Collection, Moorland-Spingarn Research Center, Howard University.

Macdonald, Dwight. "Masscult and Midcult." In *Against the American Grain: Essays on the Effects of Mass Culture*, 3–78. New York: Random House, 1962.

McElvaine, Robert. *The Great Depression: America, 1929–1941.* New York: Times Books, 1984.

McHenry, Elizabeth. *Forgotten Readers: Recovering the Lost History of African American Literary Societies.* Durham, N.C.: Duke University Press, 2002.

McKay, Claude. Letter to Josephine Herbst. 18 August 1924. Josephine Herbst Collection, Beinecke Library, Yale University.

Madigan, Mark, ed. *Keeping Fires Night and Day: Selected Letters of Dorothy Canfield Fisher.* Columbia: University of Missouri Press, 1993.

———. "Willa Cather and Dorothy Canfield Fisher: Rift, Reconciliation, and *One of Ours.*" *Cather Studies* 1 (1990): 115–129.

Marcuse, Herbert. *The Aesthetic Dimension: Toward a Critique of Marxist Aesthetics.* Boston: Beacon, 1978.

Menand, Louis. *The Metaphysical Club: A Story of Ideas in America.* New York: Farrar, Straus and Giroux, 2001.

Mills, Margaret Bailey. Letter to Dorothy Canfield Fisher. 20 February 1931. Fan Letters, Dorothy Canfield Fisher Collection, Bailey/Howe Library, University of Vermont.

Morley, Christopher. *The Haunted Bookshop.* New York: Grosset & Dunlap, 1919.

Morrisson, Mark S. *The Poetics of Fascism: Ezra Pound, T. S. Eliot, Paul de Man.* Oxford: Oxford University Press, 1996.

———. *The Public Face of Modernism: Little Magazines, Audiences, and Reception.* Madison: University of Wisconsin Press, 2001.

Newson, Earl. Letter to Pearl Buck. 23 January 1931. John Day Collection, Princeton University Library.

Nolte, William H., ed. *H.L. Mencken's Smart Set Criticism.* Ithaca, N.Y.: Cornell University Press, 1968.

Overton, Grant. *The Women Who Make Our Novels.* (1918) New York: Dodd, Mead, 1926.

Parchesky, Jennifer. "Melodramas of Everyday Life: Fiction, Film, and the Making of Middle America." Diss., Duke University.

Pearce, Charles. Letter to Josephine Herbst. 25 March, 5 July, and 11 October 1933; 14 December 1934; 29 July 1938. Josephine Herbst Collection. Beinecke Library, Yale University.

Piacentino, Edward. *T. S. Stribling: Pioneer Realist in Modern Southern Literature.* Lanham, Md.: University Press of America, 1988.

Radway, Janice. *A Feeling for Books: The Book-of-the-Month Club, Literary Taste, and Middle-Class Desire.* Chapel Hill: University of North Carolina Press, 1997.

———. "On the Gender of the Middlebrow Consumer." *Southern Atlantic Quarterly* 93.4 (Fall 1994): 874–894.

Reader Report. *Rope of Gold.* Book-of-the-Month Club Archive, 1939, Library of Congress.

Reader Report. *Native Son.* Book-of-the-Month Club Archive, 1940, Library of Congress.

[Review of *The Executioner Waits.*] *Book-of-the-Month Club News.* November 1934.

[Review of *The Executioner Waits.*] *Carolina Magazine.* Reviews, Herbst Collection. Beinecke Library, Yale University.

[Review of *The Executioner Waits.*] *Common Sense.* Reviews, Herbst Collection. Beinecke Library, Yale University.

[Review of *The Executioner Waits.*] *Opinion* December 1934. Reviews, Herbst Collection. Beinecke Library, Yale University.

[Review of *The Executioner Waits.*] *Salden.* Reviews, Herbst Collection. Beinecke Library, Yale University.

[Review of *The Executioner Waits.*] *The Waldorf-Astoria Magazine.* 10 November 1934. Reviews, Herbst Collection. Beinecke Library, Yale University.

[Review of *The Good Earth.*] *New Statesman and Nation* 16 May 1931: 430.

[Review of *There Is Confusion*]. *Booklist* (July 1924): 378.

[Review of *There Is Confusion*]. *New Republic* 9 July 1924: 192.

[Review of *There Is Confusion*]. *New York Times Book Section,* 13 April 1924: 9, 16.

Reynolds, Paul Revere. Letter to Dorothy Canfield. 9 February 1930; 15 January 1932. Paul Reynolds Collection. Butler Library, Columbia University.

———. *The Middle Man: Adventures of a Literary Agent.* New York: Morrow, 1972.

Rideout, Walter. *The Radical Novel in the United States, 1900–1954.* Cambridge: Harvard University Press, 1956.

Rosenblatt, Louise M. *Literature as Exploration.* New York: Appleton Century, 1938.

Rubin, Joan Shelley. *The Making of Middlebrow Culture.* Chapel Hill: University of North Carolina Press, 1992.

Salter, Paul, and Jack Librome. "Dewey, Russell, and Cohen: Why They Are Anti Communist (Concluded)." *New Masses* 24 July 1934.

Satterfield, Jay. *"The World's Best Books": Taste, Culture, and the Modern Library.* Amherst: University of Massachusetts Press, 2002.

Scadura, Jani, and Michael Thurston, eds. *Modernism, Inc.: Body, Memory, Capital.* New York: New York University Press, 2001.

Scott, Bonnie Kime. *The Gender of Modernism: A Critical Anthology.* Bloomington: Indiana University Press: 1990.

Sklar, Martin J. *The Corporate Reconstruction of American Capitalism, 1890–1916: The Market, the Law, and Politics.* New York: Cambridge University Press, 1988.

Smith, Bernard. "Another Liberal Collapses." *New Masses* 15 May 1934.

———. "Howells: The Genteel Radical." *Saturday Review of Literature* 11 August 1934.

Smith, Bill. "Cupid's Letter Box." *New Masses* 10 April 1934: 30.

Smith, Erin A. *Hard-Boiled: Working-Class Readers and Pulp Fiction.* Philadelphia: Temple University Press, 2000.

Snow, Walter. "A Salute to Hicks." Correspondence. *New Masses* 10 July 1934: 25.

Starkey, Marion L. "Jessie Fauset." *The Southern Workman* May 1932: 217–220.

Stowe, Harriet Beecher. *Uncle Tom's Cabin: or Life Among the Lowly.* Garden City, N.Y.: Dolphin Books, 1960.

Susman, Warren I. *Culture as History: The Transformation of American Society in the Twentieth Century.* (1984) Washington, D.C.: Smithsonian Books, 2003.

Sylvander, Carolyn Wedin. *Jessie Redmon Fauset, Black American Writer.* Troy, N.Y.: Whitston, 1981.

Tebbel, John. *A History of Publishing in the United States.* Vol. 3: *The Golden Age between Two Wars, 1920–1940.* New York: R. R. Bowker, 1978.

Tebbel, John, and Mary Ellen Zuckerman, eds. *The Magazine in America, 1741–1990.* New York: Oxford University Press, 1991.

Terrell, Mary Church. *A Colored Woman in a White World.* Intro. Nellie Y. McKay. New York: G. K. Hall, 1996.

Thornton Academy Distinguished Alumni. http://64.177.91.12/alumni/pdaglane.shtml.

Tomlinson, Susan. "Changing Meanings of Jessie Fauset." Diss., Brown University. 1998.

Tompkins, Jane. *Sensational Designs: The Cultural Work of American Fiction, 1790–1860.* New York: Oxford University Press, 1985.

Trachtenberg, Alan. *The Incorporation of America: Culture and Society in the Gilded Age.* New York: Hill and Wang, 1982.

Travis, Trysh. "Print and the Creation of Middlebrow Culture." In *Perspectives on American Book History: Artifacts and Commentary,* ed. Scott E. Casper, Joanne D. Chaison, and Jeffrey D. Groves, 339–366. Amherst:University of Massachusetts Press, 2002.

Turner, Catherine. *Marketing Modernism between the Two World Wars.* Amherst: University of Massachusetts Press, 2003.

"Upton Sinclair's Threat." *New Masses* 11 September 1934.

Van Slyke, Beren. Letter to Dorothy Canfield Fisher. 19 July 1931. Fan Letters. Dorothy Canfield Fisher Collection, Bailey/Howe Library, University of Vermont.

Wall, Cheryl. *Women of the Harlem Renaissance.* Bloomington: Indiana University Press, 1995.

Walsh, Richard. Letter to Pearl Buck. 25 February, 7 May, 3 July, and 6 August 1931; 27 February 1933. John Day Collection, Princeton University Library.

———. Transcript of radio broadcast, dated 1932, contained in Walsh to Pearl Buck correspondence, November 22–December 16, 1932, John Day Collection, Princeton University Library.

Walton, Eda. Review of *The Good Earth. The Nation* 13 May 1931: 534.

Warshow, Robert. "The Legacy of the 30's." In *The Immediate Experience: Movies, Comics, Theatre, and Other Aspects of Popular Culture,* 33–48.Garden City, N.Y.: Doubleday, 1962.

Washington, Ida H. *Dorothy Canfield Fisher: A Biography.* Shelburne, Vt.: New England Press, 1982.

Weinstein, James. *The Corporate Ideal in the Liberal State, 1900–1918.* Boston: Beacon Press, 1968.

West, James L.W., III. *American Authors and the Literary Marketplace since 1900.* Philadelphia: University of Pennsylvania Press, 1988.

White, William Allen. "The Other Side of Main Street." *Collier's Weekly* 30 July 1921: 16–19.

Widle, Mrs. Ernest J. Letter to Dorothy Canfield Fisher. 26 June 1943. Fan Letters. Dorothy Canfield Fisher Collection, Bailey/Howe Library, University of Vermont.

Williams, Deborah Lindsay. *Not in Sisterhood: Edith Wharton, Willa Cather, Zona Gale, and the Politics of Female Authorship.* New York: Palgrave, 2001.

Wilson, Christopher. *The Labor of Words: Literary Professionalism in the Progressive Era.* Athens: University of Georgia Press, 1985.

Woollcott, Alexander. "Shouts and Murmurs: The Vanishing Lady." *New Yorker* 13 August 1932: 22.

Wycoff, Elizabeth. "A Neglected Bestseller." *Bookman* 74 (September 1931): 40–44.

Yates, Elizabeth. *Pebble in a Pool: The Widening Circles of Dorothy Canfield Fisher's Life.* New York: Dutton, 1958.

Yutang, Lin. Review of *All Men Are Brothers. China Critic* 4 January 1934.

Index